Eikona Bridge

LIVE Communication with the Autistic Species

Jason H. J. Lu, PhD

To Jianjun,
Best Wishes,
Jason Lu
2014-12-6

To everyone in the world,

but especially to Tisa, Mindy, and Ivan!

Eikona (pronounced *eye-koe-nah*) means "image" in Greek. *Eikona Bridge* aims to build a connection between children with autism and their parents, through visual means. Hopefully this bridge will help many frustrated parents and children out there. Why a Greek word, you ask? Did you know *autism* itself is a Greek word?

LIVE (rhymes with five) is an acronym which stands for Letters, Images, Voice, and Experience. Together, these four elements make up the essence of the Eikona Bridge.

CONTENTS

Chapter 4 – Pro-Picture Children ·················· **111**

ACKNOWLEDGMENTS

I have too many people to thank. To my wife Tisa for her persistence. To my children, Mindy and Ivan, for their life stories and for their laughter. To my nephews Tin and Pi, and to my brother-in-law Pham, for broadening my understanding of people with autism. To my awesome parents, sister, and brother. Daddy, you are the inspiration for the lullaby at the end of this book...you are the "really old, old man." To my in-laws, all too many to list out here. To my teachers, professors, classmates, and colleagues: you have seeded in me the tools for understanding autism. To all the therapists and teachers who helped Mindy and Ivan: thanks so much for your love and dedication. To the people of California: thanks for providing assistance to families with children with autism.

And I thank you, the reader, for making an effort to understand us, the members of the autistic species. I truly appreciate it.

PROLOGUE

My wife told me to write this book. That's all I can say.

Seriously, I have no autism research background. Autism research is a field full of domain experts. I don't know their names. I have no idea about the current literature. I have not interacted personally with that many children or adults with autism. I have also never written a book, and to make things even more interesting, English is not my native language. It takes blind chutzpah to step into this field, explain to people what autism is, and on top of that, tell them what to do. I must be crazy, right? My only consolation is my wife must be crazier, because she is the one who kept pushing me to write this book.

I have to give my wife credit for her persistence. She knows I have a message to deliver. She knows I understand my two children with autism better than anyone else in the world. She knows I speak their language. And she truly believes that I can help other children with autism out there as well. Whether her blind faith is misplaced or not, you will have to judge.

My wife's motto is: "It takes an autistic person to understand another autistic person." She is not an autistic person, so at times I wonder her true intentions behind her motto.... I chuckle to myself: maybe what she *really* means is that she will take the children to school and do all the cooking at home, and that in return she expects me to do all the work...to understand our children! I think I may have gotten the short end of the stick! But more seriously, after I started to write this book and do some research, I found out that many things I have been telling my wife all these years are echoed by other people with autism. Autism is no longer a newly discovered condition: many of those children first diagnosed with autism are now adults, and they have let the world know their opinions. For instance, I have found out that I am not the only one who doesn't want to be "cured" of autism. I have found out that many people don't believe that autism is a "disorder," let alone a "disability." I have found out that many believe that autism means just a different way of thinking, learning, and communicating. I have found out other people also believe that repetitive behaviors should not be suppressed. And most preciously, I have found out that I am not the only one who believes that autism is part of human evolution. So a consistent picture of autism is emerging, thanks to the input of adults with autism. Unfortunately, a lot of misconceptions and bad advice persist out there, coming mostly from people who are not autistic. So I believe my wife is right; it does take an autistic person to understand another autistic person.

My wife and I have two children, Mindy and Ivan. Their names have been altered to protect their privacy. Some of the drawings in the book have been edited for the same purpose.

Mindy and Ivan are here on earth to make people happy. They were happy babies. My in-laws always told us that we were very lucky, that other babies were not as easygoing. This is perhaps hard to believe, because both Mindy and Ivan are clinically diagnosed with autism.

Mindy and Ivan have different kinds of autism. I had an easy connection with Mindy right away. I could understand her almost by reflex. We have the same kind of autism. While other people struggled to understand Mindy and to communicate with her, I had no problem whatsoever. However, with Ivan it was a different story. For the first two and a half years of Ivan's life, I couldn't understand him. I couldn't communicate with him, and there was a distance between us, a distance so big that my wife had to ask me, "Do you even realize that he is your son?" I think I was trying to escape. I was lost. I thought I knew how to interact with my kids because I understood Mindy so well, but obviously I was a failure with Ivan,

2

and I couldn't face reality. With Mindy, I did not need to think; I just needed to follow my instincts. With Ivan, my reflexes were all off the mark. I racked my brain thinking about how to approach him. It was hard work and it was frustrating. With Mindy, I drew pictures, and she loved them. I taught her almost everything through pictures. But Ivan showed zero interest in my drawings. I couldn't teach him anything that way. At the age of two and half, he did not even call me Papa, despite my nonstop effort to relate to him. Ivan also had more behavior issues, and cried more easily. Based on my own experience growing up, and on research I conducted, reading Dr. Temple Grandin's books about autism, I was certain that children with autism must be visual. Yet Ivan did not respond to pictures. What was going on? All my understanding about children with autism was falling apart. And I was losing my son.

I loved my children with all my heart, but that was obviously not enough. I need to love them with my head, too, I told myself. So I started to think about what clues I may have missed. Sometimes I just sat in the family room and let my mind wander. One of those late nights I turned on the big-screen TV to watch some meaningless shows, but random thoughts were floating in my head. I thought about Mindy and Ivan, about how diametrically opposite they were to each other. I directed my eyesight towards the big screen TV...its rectangular shape reminded me of the phase-space coordinate system. Then I imagined Mindy on the horizontal side of the TV screen, and Ivan on the vertical side. Horizontal *vs.* vertical...coordinate *vs.* momentum...static *vs.* dynamic...quiet *vs.* hyperactive...column *vs.* row...object *vs.* aspect...Mindy *vs.* Ivan...picture *vs.*...picture *vs.*...picture *vs.*...video?!

It all changed the day when I understood Ivan: yes, Ivan was visual, but he was a video-memory person, not a picture-memory person! It surely helped that I learned about Fourier transforms in my calculus class some thirty years ago. After I found out the nature of Ivan's memory, things developed really fast. Finally I started to have a string of successes with him. He learned to look at my drawings, learned to read, and learned to call me Papa! Best of all, we became closer friends. I was finally behaving like a father. It took real work, real effort on my part to understand Ivan, but it was all worth it. Nothing was more rewarding than when I could finally communicate with my child. In short, I learned to speak his language.

So this book is about success stories. Yes, success stories, plural. Success with Mindy and success with Ivan. It's about a family coming together, and having fun along the way. It was hard work. Sometimes I spent days and nights, nonstop, drawing flowchart diagrams, analyzing radio circuits, reviewing equations on Fourier transforms and operator calculus, trying to find explanations and solutions by drawing analogies from mathematics. And today I can proudly say I did not give up on my son. My wife was amazed that I could look at mathematical equations and come up with solutions to communicate with Ivan. In response to her amazement, I could only reply, "It takes an autistic person to understand another autistic person."

I will tell you another success story that is even more personal. One day, after this book was mostly finished, my wife turned to me and said, "You know, before you started to write the book, I really didn't know you. It was only after you wrote the book that I came to understand you." For the first time in my life, there was a person who understood me. That was a most heartwarming moment. I asked my wife, "But didn't you say it takes an autistic person to understand another autistic person?" She just smiled and said, "I guess I am becoming autistic, too."

So, I have a message to share. And I hope other families with children with autism can benefit from this message and grow stronger together. My message is: Autism is a communication problem. You solve the communication problem, and everything else will fall in place.

Tossing Ivan into the air, so that he can "fall in place." No worries, I always catch him on the way down. "A la one, a la two, a la three!" is our way of saying "ready, set, go!" We welcome you to our story.

1

BACKGROUND

A Different Species

While looking for a suitable preschool for my daughter, one day I took her to a new school for a tryout. The first part of the morning session was not very structured because the school had a Montessori component, and children were supposed to do things a bit on their own. While my daughter was busy coloring, I was getting bored observing. Just when I thought nothing much was happening, a little boy came over and started to talk to me. He brought me a book on reptiles, and told me about crocodiles. His speech was not very clear, but he was obviously eager to show me things. He went on to talk about trains. I grabbed a piece of paper and drew a picture of a toy train on a track. Then he told me there was a tunnel, and I drew a little mountain with a tunnel. Then he told me about the zoo and his camping trip, and that he toasted marshmallows over the campfire. I drew some more pictures on the sheet of paper about camping, crocodiles, and other animals. Our "conversation" went on for a while, until the paper was full, and then he said the paper needed to go into his "art folder." The boy was glued to me for so long that I felt like I was working as his teacher, and I almost forgot that I was there to observe my own daughter.

The observation session turned out to be longer than I could stay for—I had to go to work, after all. So I called my wife and asked her to come over to replace me. After my wife arrived, I told her that I didn't know why, but there was this little boy that was glued to me all morning. As a matter of fact, even when he was outside doing a group activity, he would still turn his head to check on me, as if he wanted to talk some more. I told my wife that the boy might have autism. She just smiled at me and said, "You guys from the same species can sense each other."

No, I don't think I "sense" people with autism any better than others do, but my wife would always tell other people, "It takes an autistic person to understand another autistic person." Truth be told, it has been tough for my wife to live with three people on the autism spectrum: me and our two children. I give her a lot of credit for her patience.

Frankly, I did not pay attention to autism until one nephew on my wife's side of the family got the diagnosis. Later, his younger brother was also diagnosed with autism. Then my daughter followed, and then my son. Another nephew was diagnosed with autism after that. Then I found out that my workplace was full of people with children with autism: at least four more cases from my immediate co-workers. When people tell me that autism has reached epidemic proportions, I tell them, yes, I know.

Epidemic proportions, yes. An epidemic? It is not. As someone on the spectrum, I dislike thinking about autism as an illness or a disorder. After all, I am a fully functional person. I earned a PhD degree from a top school. I work, make a living, am married, and am raising a family.

I communicated so well with my daughter that I found it hard to understand why other people had difficulty communicating with her. To me, my daughter's diagnosis did not mean that she was less capable than anyone else. As a matter of fact, her reading skills were way ahead of her peers. Mindy just communicated in a different way from typical people: she was visual, not verbal. So was I: visual, not verbal. Or as I put it, "Like father, like daughter."

If autism is not an illness, then what is it? Let's see: It is genetic in nature, meaning every single cell of the person is affected by the same autistic genes. It can propagate from one generation to the next. These are pretty much the characteristics of a species, or sub-species, if you like. An autism diagnosis can be overwhelming for families, and parents may find it hard to adapt to supporting a child with autism. Yet, I never found myself sad or overwhelmed by our situation. I was not in denial, either. I was keenly aware that children with autism mean a great deal of work. But I kept telling myself that the payoff was going to be totally worth it. Besides, I couldn't help but feel like, "Hey, it's my species, and we are taking over the world!" So I thought I might as well get some fun out of it. And what fun I have had! Seeing the children grow and develop has made all the effort worthwhile. No, I have never shed a single teardrop over my children's conditions. Instead, I have had tons of laughter with my happy children. Happy children with big smiles.

On the subject of happy children, I am not exaggerating. Both Mindy and Ivan have repeatedly received compliments from teachers and other parents as being happy and easy children. This is especially so with Mindy. Teachers and other parents often tell us, "Mindy is always happy!" and one teacher with a child herself even said to my wife, "That's so unfair. You guys have two children, and they are both always happy."

Of course, my wife and I are lucky to have high-functioning children with autism. But seeing how some parents treat their children with autism makes my heart break. Many children with autism have special talents and can become successful adults. Yet, parents and teachers may not always achieve to communicate with these children, despite best intentions. Some of these children become discouraged, and their hidden potential remains locked away. If these children miss out during their prime time for learning, they risk remaining permanently underdeveloped.

I can't speak for all cases of autism, as the spectrum is wide, but I believe I can speak for the majority of cases. I would urge parents to stop searching for miracle cures: autism is not a vaccine problem, and it is not a diet problem. The children are fine. I would ask parents to shift their energy from "correcting" their children's behavior, to spending more time communicating with them...in these children's language. I would like parents to always keep two things in mind: one, children with autism are smart; and two, they are visual, not verbal. We need to get to them through their eyes, not through their ears. One day these children will be able to communicate verbally and think verbally, but until then, our job is to build the bridge—the Eikona Bridge.

In What Language Do You Think?

English is my fourth language. I was born in Asia and spent my adolescent years growing up in South America. Because my brother and I were the only Asian children in our high school, we were treated like exotic animals.

I remember in my early teen years, my classmates once asked me how many languages I spoke. "Three," I told them. (Back then I still did not know English.) Then one of them asked me, "So, in what language do you think?"

I was startled. I really did not know what he meant. In my mind, that was a very odd question. Why would anyone need a language to think? I certainly did not think in any particular language. It was silent inside my brain. I told them that I didn't think in any particular language, I just *thought*. Sure, I could speak three languages and I constructed sentences on the fly when I spoke, but I did not use any language to think.

I did not realize that I was different from the other children. I assumed that everyone's thinking process was the same as mine. I did not realize that, while I was thinking in pictures, other children were thinking in sentences.

Only when I was around seventeen years old did I start to think verbally. Gradually I realized that there was a voice creeping inside my brain. And with verbal thinking there was no turning back, for once I started it, I lost the ability to think purely in pictures. At least, my brain was not quiet anymore. Depending on the setting, I was thinking in this or that language. So yes, I started using all my languages to think.

When I started to look into autism, I ran into Dr. Temple Grandin's book, *Thinking in Pictures*. After reading it, I came to realize that I myself was autistic! Sure, I was verbal and did not have speech delay, so I would probably be on the Asperger, or lighter side, of the autism spectrum. But I finally found out who I was and why I was different from my friends. I started to understand why I communicated and behaved in certain ways. I still behave in certain autistic ways today. I can't change it. It's who I am.

Pictures, Pictures, and More Pictures

I was not particularly skillful at drawing pictures, but I loved to doodle. I loved simple figures and simple colors. I preferred watching cartoons to movies with human actors. Even when I was in my PhD program, I still doodled. I just loved to stare at my simple drawings. I managed to sneak a drawing into my PhD thesis, which I reproduce on the next page. There you go: a desperate cry from someone from another species that was being morphed into a normal human.

So, there you have it: I was drawing, long before I knew anything about autism. Looking at it today, I realize that back then I also must have vaguely sensed I was different from "normal humans." I was autistic. I just didn't know it.

When Mindy was about two years old, she still did not talk and did not walk. She was such a cutie pie, but soon enough we realized that she was falling behind. Our pediatrician told us to contact a specialist, and Mindy started to receive ABA (Applied Behavioral Analysis) services at around two and half years of age.

Picture from my PhD thesis

Back then Mindy wasn't even calling me "Papa." That would still take her another eight months or so. The traditional ABA approach taught children to say sentences like, "I want..." but since Mindy wasn't saying words, I further shortened it into "me..." I also suspected that Mindy would take visual input better than aural input, so I made three video clips with some photos of Mindy to teach her to say "me down," "me out," and "me car": basically shorthand for "I want to get down (from the high chair)," "I want to get outside the safety fence," and "I want to ride the cozy coupe (a toy car)." I used a yellow Pac-Man-like icon overlaying the photo pictures when the word "me" was sounded out, and yellow arrows for "down" and "out," and a yellow vehicle icon for "car." Mindy definitely enjoyed watching the video clips, but she wasn't echoing the "sentences." So I thought the technique wasn't working.

"ME DOWN"
Notice the visual cues: a Pac-Man-like icon for "ME," and an arrow for "DOWN." The actual video used photos.

One day, my wife called me at work and she sounded extremely worried. She told me that Mindy's eyes were swollen and that it was an emergency situation. I rushed home and sure enough, Mindy had horribly swollen eyes. I took her to the emergency room immediately. It turned out that Mindy had a bad case of conjunctivitis. The nurses had to give her an eye flush, so we needed to immobilize her. One nurse held Mindy's legs, I held Mindy's arms, and another nurse did the flushing. Of course, that was extremely traumatic to a two-year-old child. Mindy was crying her lungs out and tried to kick as hard as she could, and suddenly she started to scream "ME DOWN! ME DOWN! ME DOWN!" She was in such a pitiful state, but I couldn't help breaking out in a big smile—she did understand my video clips! That made my day. I was still concerned about her eye condition, of course, but it was so delightful to hear her say the right words at the right moment! The ME DOWN moment was unforgettable. It gave me proof that Mindy was a visual person, which marked the way she would learn things from then on.

Mindy did not talk, but curiously enough, she loved the alphabet. Around 18 months of age, she could recognize all the letters of the alphabet. Lower case and upper case. And later she also learned to read cursive, pretty much on her own. When Mindy was late in talking, all the grandparents got worried, and pressure built up around the house. Frankly, many of the comments weren't helpful at all. Ignorance about autism abounded. People unfamiliar with autism tended to equate it with mental retardation.

When Mindy was two and half years of age, one day, just for the fun of it, I started to teach her how to read simple words. I spelled the word CAT on her magnetic drawing board and told her: "C là kuh, kuh, kuh, A là ah, ah, ah, T là tuh, tuh, tuh, C-A-T là kuh-ah-tuh, cat!" ("Là" is the Vietnamese word for "is".) I did not expect her to understand what the whole exercise was about, but surprisingly, she picked it up right away, and repeated the whole exercise. She pointed to each letter, and said: "C là kuh, kuh, kuh, A là ah, ah, ah, T là tuh, tuh, tuh, C-A-T là kuh-ah-tuh, cat!" Startled, I went on to teach her CAR, and DOG, and she picked them up right away, too. The next day, I wrote down CAT, and asked her what it was, and she said "cat!" I couldn't believe it. Just to make sure, I tried CAR and DOG, and sure enough, she said "car" and "dog!" I jumped up and down, and called my wife over to come check it out. We confirmed that she was reading, not just separate letters, but whole words! In a span of two days, she learned to read and sound out most letters. It only took a few more days for her to sound out digraphs like *ch*, *sh*, *cl*, and *tr*. English is far from a phonetic language, yet Mindy didn't seem to have any problem with the complex rules and the many exceptions of English spelling. Since I also spoke Spanish, I taught her Spanish words, and she picked them up without any problem. It was like magic. You threw random words at her, either in English or Spanish, and she could sound them out. I did not need to teach her that the final *e* is silent in English but not silent in Spanish. She just knew.

That was when I told myself, "All right, forget about the conventional wisdom…Mindy can't talk yet, but I am going to teach her to read!" Talking could wait. Reading was a more natural way of communicating with her. The door was now open. Mindy was behind in virtually all developmental areas: she was a late talker, late walker, and she had weak muscle tone. But when it came to reading, she was two years ahead of her peers! That made all the difference: now I had something to hold on to. I had hope: Mindy's brain was OK!

I bought a magnetic drawing board, one of those that you could draw on and then erase by sliding a knob. Every night I would draw some pictures for her. In the beginning, I only labeled words on the side, and then later I started to add speech bubbles like the ones in comic books. When my wife wanted me to tell Mindy what to do, I would draw pictures for Mindy, often with speech bubbles, and turn those drawings into a story. Mindy loved pictures. Even years later, she would still come to me and say, "Papa, I want pictures," or "Papa, let's draw some pictures," or "Papa, we need to draw some pictures."

That was how Mindy learned many things in her early childhood: through pictures. I shared my "method" with Mindy's ABA therapists, and soon everyone was drawing pictures for Mindy. Pictures did not work for everything, though. For instance, Mindy's potty training process took forever, and pictures did not help a bit. I even made a peeing honey bear toy to show to Mindy, but it did not help either. So the visual approach certainly had its limits, and I really appreciated the help we received from Mindy's ABA services.

I read *Calvin and Hobbes* to Mindy. It is a comic book series with a little boy named Calvin and his stuffed toy tiger named Hobbes. Mindy's visual learning skills were superb: she had an uncanny ability to understand characters' emotions in comic books. She absorbed information both from the written sentences and from the comic drawings. She also imitated many of Calvin's travesties, much to my wife's despair. My wife blamed the comic book for Mindy's screaming and other naughty behaviors such as refusing to eat or take a bath. But I told my wife to let Mindy do it, that it was just a phase. I also told my wife, "Aren't you glad that Mindy can protest and talk now?" And my wife had to agree.

When Mindy was four years old, I was reading *Diary of a Wimpy Kid* to her, a book that was meant for children age eight to twelve. I bought the book because there weren't many books written from a first-person perspective out there that also had drawings. I wanted books with "template" sentences that Mindy could copy and use, and the choices were meager: authors just did not target children with autism. With the books we did find, and the pictures we drew, plus plenty of help from ABA and school, Mindy learned to talk.

If You Have Met One Child with Autism...

There is a well-known saying in the autism community: "If you have met one child with autism, then you have met one child with autism." It is very true. Each child with autism is different. Due to the case of Mindy, my son Ivan received early intervention at age of 15 months, and was confirmed with autism when he was age of three. Earlier, both of their cousins were also confirmed with autism. Yet, all four children were different.

One would think that with the insight we gained from Mindy, dealing with Ivan would be easier. That was not the case. Ivan and Mindy often were diametrically opposite to each other. Mindy liked to be quiet and sit down to read. Ivan couldn't stay still for two seconds. What worked for Mindy did not work for Ivan. For one thing, Ivan couldn't stand staring at pictures. Static pictures meant nothing to him.

The ABA therapists kept reassuring me that Ivan was making progress. His attention span was getting longer. We also realized that Ivan was a good problem solver. He was thinking two steps ahead, sometimes three steps ahead. For instance, he would get a chair to reach something like an electric toothbrush, and if we placed the chair somewhere else, he would get the chair from the other room, drag it all the way to the bathroom, and then climb on top of the chair to get the toothbrush.

So Ivan was also smart, but in a different way. Ivan could solve problems that Mindy could not. But I felt like I still couldn't communicate effectively with Ivan. I always fell back to Mindy. With Mindy, I did not need to think—I understood her perfectly. She had my kind of autism. Ivan was a strange case to me. I couldn't understand him and couldn't communicate with him. I knew I was losing him; we were like strangers.

In the chair and toothbrush example, clearly Ivan was visual, too. He was correlating geometric positioning of objects with problem solving. Ivan was a keen observer. Whenever I worked with something mechanical, be it a computer, vacuum cleaner, screwdriver, or label printer, he would always pay very close attention to what I was doing.

So if Ivan was visual, but not interested in pictures, then what was going on? Then it hit me—he was interested in movies! That is, video clips. Ivan couldn't stand dealing with static pictures. Pictures or drawings had no information for him. If Mindy was static, Ivan was dynamic: only things in motion carried information for Ivan.

Then I remembered something from my calculus class. Mindy and Ivan were like Fourier transforms of each other. (Pardon me for my monologue here using technical jargon. Please refer to the Glossary at the end of this book for the explanation of the technical terms.) Yes, coordinate space versus momentum space. If Mindy captured and stored information in the coordinate space inside her brain, then Ivan was capturing and storing information in the momentum space. These two children simply stored information differently. If we borrow an analogy from matrix theory, one of them stored information in columns, and the other stored information in rows. At the end of the day, both would learn the same things, but their approaches were destined to be different.

So I started to make videos for Ivan, and could indeed confirm that he was paying attention. But for the important things I wanted to teach him, I couldn't make animated movies easily. So what could I do? For instance, if I wanted to teach Ivan vocabulary words such as "happy" and "sad", or "nice" and "scary," or to teach Ivan about wearing seatbelt, I couldn't afford the time to make sophisticated animations. I could draw pictures and overlay words on images, but true animations were out of my reach.

I racked my brain thinking about the problem. I had things I wanted to teach Ivan, but they were all in static pictures. After all, like Mindy, I was a picture-memory person, not a video-memory person. Yet Ivan was only taking in dynamic videos. That was why Ivan was not learning from pictures. How could I rearrange my information in such a way that Ivan would understand and absorb it?

I noticed that Ivan's attention span for static pictures did not go beyond three to five seconds. I needed to take advantage of those precious three to five seconds. Then I remembered the "convolution" formula from Fourier Analysis. In the "convolution" formula, one basically intertwined two input signals together. It's a technique widely used in radio signal transmission, where it is better known as "modulation," as in the terms AM/FM, standing for Amplitude Modulation and Frequency Modulation. So, it was now clear what I needed to do: I could interlace static images with Ivan's favorite videos. For instance, he liked to watch the *Twinkle, Twinkle Little Star* video and a dinosaur video. I could insert some static frames containing my drawings into the videos! I started with cartoon drawings of the family members: Papa, Mami, Mindy, and Ivan. After the main video started to play, a character would appear for three seconds, then the main video continued, then another character popped up for three seconds, followed by the main video, etc. I called this technique "doing the commercials," because that's what TV stations do: they run a main program to keep you glued to the TV set, and then insert commercials for those "important messages" from their sponsors. Another technique was to have a sequence of real-person pictures gradually morphing into cartoon drawings. This might sound fancy, but there were several websites that provided cartoon transformation of real pictures, free of charge, so it was quite easy to implement.

And that was how Ivan learned to call me "Papa" and recognized my drawing for the "Papa" character. It was a bit time consuming. I made three video clips, and each video clip took me two or three hours to make. But the technique worked. The good thing about video clips is that you can play them over and over again. Children with autism love repetition. All things considered, this was still the fastest way to teach Ivan to call me "Papa," because all the other techniques we tried previously did not work.

I know that not everyone knows how to edit movies and make videos. Besides, it is very time consuming. And while the video and "commercial" technique worked, how could I teach Ivan when I was busy and did not have time to make videos?

I realized that the essential idea of "modulation" or "placing commercials" did not need to be video-based. For instance, Ivan liked to play with balls, dinosaurs, and cars. I learned that it was possible to schedule a main activity for Ivan. We did the main activity with him, but we interlaced it with "commercials," where we taught him the things we wanted to teach him.

I can't emphasize enough the need to have ABA therapists working closely with parents. We were lucky that we had a good case supervisor who was willing to listen to us and adopt our suggestions. I would urge parents to seek out good case supervisors. It makes a big difference. Mindy's therapists started to draw pictures for her because they were willing to listen to us, and adopt our methods. As for Ivan, when I showed my videos for Ivan to the case supervisor, she understood what I was trying to do, but frowned at how she could make it practical. Videos are great, but surely we couldn't ask all ABA therapists to become expert video editors and producers. I reassured her that video clips were only a temporary means. I was trying to get Ivan familiarized with picture drawings. Once Ivan became familiar with pictures, then we could proceed to teach him with pictures, just like with Mindy. As it turned out, I only made a total of about six videos before I realized that Ivan was already able to look at and follow my drawings! Hooray, another door was now open!

Ultimately, the goal is to get Ivan to communicate verbally. But it is not a simple trip from point A to point B. It is more like a road trip to Chilean Patagonia: the road is bumpy, and numerous bridges/ferries are needed along the way. Ivan needs to learn first from video clips, then from pictures, and then from reading. Then he will learn to generate his own manual-visual outputs. And only after all these steps will he become truly verbal. The goal of the video approach is to help Ivan adapt his video memory to his picture memory. It's the very first bridge. It's the start of a beautiful journey with breathtaking scenery at every stretch.

Ivan could have easily been dismissed as someone with hyperactivity or attention deficit disorder. But after understanding the way he captured information, and the way he stored information in his brain,

I started to figure out ways to communicate with him, ways to help him learn efficiently. I spent a great amount of time thinking about solutions. It was a lot of trial and error. Ivan did not have my type of autism, so I needed to work much harder with him. But I gradually came to understand him. Best of all, we became friends. He realized that someone in this world was speaking his language!

Mindy and Ivan were both smart children, but they needed to be communicated with differently from "typical" children. ("Typical children" is technical jargon in the early childhood development community, and it generally means "normal, non-autistic" children.) Once we found out how to open the doors to communicate with Mindy and Ivan, they learned really fast. I believe that most children with autism have hidden talents, and we just need to find a way to unlock their intellectual power. The key is to remember that we need to go through their eyes, not through their ears.

So my advice to parents of children with autism is this: build the bridges first. Start communicating. If your children are not listening to you, do not get frustrated and blame them. Children with autism do not communicate through their ears. Your words are noises to them. You might as well speak in Klingon to them because they won't understand you through your words. Verbal skills will have to wait. Communicate with your children through images and videos. Know where the doors to their brains are. Build the foundation, build the bridges, and one day they will surprise you with their talents.

I would urge parents to stop treating autism as a disorder. To me, there is nothing wrong with these children. They are not sick, and they certainly don't need to be "cured." Sure, a special diet helps—I myself can feel the difference—and our children do follow a special diet. But diet alone does not address the root of the communication problem. The autistic genes are present in each and every cell of their bodies. You can't modify the genetic composition of each and every cell, so stop pretending that it is a medical problem (except in some very severe cases). Instead, treat your children as people from a different human species. Learn to communicate with them. Give them dignity, and have loads of fun along the way. It's a great deal of work, but the payoff is far greater. I like this quote from Dr. Temple Grandin, from *The Way I See It: A Personal Look at Autism & Asperger's*:

> "If all the genes and other factors that cause autism were eliminated, the world would be populated by very social people who would accomplish very little."

Save the children with autism, because one day, they will be the ones who will save the world.

Autism: Epidemic?

One day, my brother-in-law was chatting with his wife. She said to him, "Jason says that autism is part of human evolution, and that this 'new species' is slowly gaining an upper hand over the 'normal' species." My brother-in-law laughed and said, "But they are already the majority! Look at our two families—they are five, and we are three!" He meant that all four children and I were autistic, and that he, his wife, and my wife were typical: that made it five against three.

I don't know the true prevalence of autism, but the official statistics in the United States keep climbing up. I searched a bit on the Internet (from an ABC News article on March 29, 2012, and a Huffington Post article on March 20, 2013) and found out that:

- In the year 2002, the prevalence of autism was estimated to be 1 in 150 children.
- In the year 2006, the number changed to 1 in 110 children.
- In the year 2012, the number was updated to 1 in 88 children.
- In the year 2013, the prevalence of parent-reported cases was 1 in 50 children, in survey study done by Centers for Disease Control and Prevention.

Of course, a standard disclaimer applies: we don't really know whether autism has always been present at this level, or whether the increasing rates simply reflect better diagnosis (or over-diagnosis, as some say). Still, the figures should put everyone on the lookout and raise proper awareness of this condition. In a span of a decade, the incidence rate basically tripled. At this rate, and if we want to exaggerate, we can say that in another generation (or in 30 years, in 2043), children with autism will become the majority. Of course, this is playing Hollywood-style special effects with numbers, just to catch people's attention. Still, chances are high that you will personally know someone with autism, if you don't already. And there is no exaggeration there.

People may be concerned about so many "mutants" around them. They wonder what is going to happen. They wonder what will become of our society. Well, as always, what seemed abnormal once upon a time will become the new "normal" when people get used to it. Once, it was abnormal for humans to wear clothing and now everyone wears clothing. Once, it was abnormal for humans to go to school, and now everyone is encouraged to go to school. Autism is no different.

My position is, with proper special education, we stand to gain from putting extra effort into raising our special-needs children, because they are special. In the case of autism, I strongly believe that each of these children have hidden talents that go beyond what typical children can do. I believe children with autism can solve problems that we currently cannot solve, and they hold the key to the survival of the human race in the future. I also believe that people with autism hold values that are beneficial to the entire human race. Whether all this is true or not, it's what I have chosen to believe, and it's the way I will frame my interactions with children with autism.

Autism: Weakness or Strength?

When I was about ten years old, there was a community fair in our town. One of the events was a "tri-generational relay," where family members from three generations competed in a relay race. It was a lot of fun. The problem was, my grandfather had my dad around age thirty. My dad had me around age thirty also. Compared to other families, I was the youngest kid in the race. All the other children were middle or high schoolers. At the same time, my grandfather was the oldest grandpa in the race. As for my dad, his day job was sitting behind a desk and talking to clients, so there's not much muscle there, either. Needless to say, our family finished last in the race, no matter how hard I ran. I was so disappointed at my dad's and my grandpa's performance, because I knew I gave my best but I felt like those two took it easy. All the same…I still remember the loud cheers I received from the crowd—they loved seeing how hard I tried next to high schoolers twice my size.

By their generation's standard, my grandpa and my dad married late. I beat both of them by a whopping stretch, because I had Mindy when I was 44 years old. Needless to say, people often mistook me for the grandfather of my own children. The last time we went on a vacation with my wife's extended family of sixteen people, one Caucasian lady was so touched that she came over and told me, "You remind me so much of my father and grandfather. It's so nice that you could spend a vacation with all your grandchildren. You know what? I will just call you Grandpa!" Good heavens, she thought that I was the patriarch of the clan. The only thing I could do was to reciprocate with a hearty smile and not tell her the truth. How could I spoil her good feeling?

There have been a lot of studies and explanations for autism. I have seen things from the interesting to the esoteric:

- That a father's age causes autism.
- That a significant fraction of children with autism undergo an unusual brain overgrowth in first year of life.
- That autism is caused by leaky gut syndrome and that gluten must be avoided at all cost.
- That the measles, mumps, rubella (MMR) vaccine causes autism.
- That air pollution is linked to autism.
- That obesity in mothers is linked to autism.
- That drinking cow milk is linked to autism.

And the list goes on. Some of the findings are interesting, some others are esoteric. As a scientist, I ask myself one question: "How do any of these studies help me communicate with my children?"

Although I agree it is important to do more research on the causes of autism (I am a scientist, remember?), none of these studies helps me with raising my children, or helping them learn efficiently. I really don't have the time to worry about the causes. I care about how to help my children be successful people when they grow up. Yes, I know a special diet helps, and we did keep our children on a special diet when they were younger. I personally still benefit from a more organic diet, but diet is not the whole story.

Among all mammals, humans are probably the weakest species when it comes to individual survival skills. In what other species do we see offspring unable to survive on their own until they are ten years old? If we had to measure survival by individual strength, humans should have been extinct a long time ago. Yet we are the most successful mammal species on earth. We became individually weak because we have strength in families, societies, and governments. In short, we live collectively. We have synergy—the whole is greater than the sum of its parts. Our individual weakness is consequence of our collective strength.

Similarly, at first sight it is easy to dismiss autism as a weakness or even an illness. But I will argue here that the truth is more complicated, and that when we look at autism more closely, it may turn out to be well in the plans of Mother Nature.

Mother Nature works with more DNA molecules than the total memory capacity of all our supercomputers combined. Evolution works in complex ways that defy our most insightful explanations. The explosion of the number of children with autism in recent years, to me, is just part of evolution. Mother Nature learns that we have families, societies, and governments to take care of our weakest ones, so she exploits this collective ability of ours to further her own agenda on evolution. From biology's point of view, other animals must be laughing at the weakness of humans. Similarly, many people look at autism as a weakness. But is that so? If it was a weakness, why wasn't it pruned out by evolution? Instead, autism is "thriving" in its own way, at a rapid rate. If we look at autism as a genetic condition, then it is gradually gaining the upper hand over the typical human species.

On this subject, I would like to share two stories I have learned about human genetics. The first story is about a genetic disease called G6PD deficiency, where the acronym stands for a mouthful: Glucose-6-Phosphate Dehydrogenase. You don't need to know the details of this disease, but it is basically a form of a horrible allergy to certain chemicals and foods (like broad beans, known also as fava beans). Now, we tend to look at an allergy as some form of weakness. However, the same genetic trait responsible for this G6PD condition is also responsible for an enhanced resistance to a common type of malaria. So in ancient times, whenever there was a malaria epidemic, the bearers of this genetic condition were the ones that were likely to survive and repopulate their clans afterward. As my wife often says, it's yin and yang: for every bad thing, there is some good that comes out of it. Life is a balance.

The second story is about genetic diversity in an adult male's sperm. It has always puzzled me that approximately 250 million spermatozoa will try to fertilize one single egg. The old theory was that this was how Mother Nature selected the healthiest (fastest) little one for the task of propagating the species. But why do we need 250 million sperm when only one ends up doing the job? That always seemed a bit odd to me. Why would Mother Nature do it in such a lopsided way?

Well, in 2012 researchers reported finding that the genetic diversity of spermatozoa within one single adult male is just as varied as the genetic diversity of the whole population. That is, at the 250-million-count scale, things are statistical. Each single male's sperm is designed to shape not only the offspring of a particular family but also the offspring of a whole society.

It's therefore a statistical game, and the male sperm carries a huge part of the responsibility for the genetic variation of our species. It needs to design itself with variations that would allow the species to survive under the most unpredictable future environments. Sure, the female genetic variation is important, too (particularly for mtDNA, or mitochondrial DNA, which is inherited solely from the mother's side), but at a 250-million-to-one ratio, the main share of the burden for genetic variation resides on the male side.

The most obvious and important example of male sperm's genetic variation is the gender of a baby: it is decided by the father's sperm, not by the mother's egg. With this example, one learns to admire how much fine-tuning there is in the design of the sperm. *Meiosis* is the process by which a normal cell is divided into two reproductive cells. One would think it is obvious from the meiosis process that the ratio of male to female babies born should be 1:1, since in this process a normal male cell with the full XY chromosome pair is split into two spermatozoa—one with the X chromosome and another with the Y chromosome. However, the truth is much more complicated. At conception, the ratio of male-to-female embryos is actually around 120:100, but male embryos are less likely to survive to full term, making the natural sex ratio at birth closer to 105:100. That's the kind of math that goes into Mother Nature's supercomputer. My point is that Mother Nature always does her own supercomputing calculation much more sophisticatedly than we can imagine.

I don't know much about the causes of autism. But I do know that in modern society people are having babies later in life. I believe autism was already statistically encoded into the human genome thousands of years ago. I am not sure about its purpose. But the modern human's lifestyle has amplified the relevance of this genetic trait. I believe Mother Nature is trying to tell us something here, and it's our job to decipher her message.

I don't know whether I am right or wrong on this, and you may even call it a positive spin or wishful thinking, but for practical purposes, I would rather think of autism as part of human evolution, as part of the human race moving forward. Sure, I know it is more work to raise children with autism. It's a lot of work. But we humans work harder than other animals to take care of our offspring. It's all part of the deal. We have the weakest youngsters in the animal kingdom, but we are the ones who send people into space, write poems, and compose symphonies. What other animals have ever achieved that? Those weak, young humans grew up and made all these achievements possible.

So, I don't view autism as a sign of weakness. I view it as a sign of strength. Children with autism need special care when they are young, but they are our future, and they will be the ones to save our world. I side with Dr. Temple Grandin on this: we need to be thankful for people with autism.

2

MATERIALS

Compared to some high-tech treatments of autism, the required supplies for Eikona Bridge are quite simple. Don't get me wrong, I am not anti-technology. I have studied science and technology and worked in these fields my whole life. However, I don't believe that spending a fortune on the latest technological gadgets is the answer to autism special education. We can't solve autism or hide our guilt by burning money. Some materials that I have successfully used and that yield excellent results are 4x6 index cards and 4x6 mini photo albums, which cost only a few dollars. Smartphones and tablet PCs are ubiquitous now, yet I often find laptops to be more effective than the new devices. Truth be told, the one device that helped Mindy most throughout her early childhood was a magnetic drawing board, which you can get for under $30. Despite my experience as a software programmer for children's educational games, I believe that software tools should only play a supplementary role for children with autism. The personal touch is a much more important component in your interaction with your child. I find simple markers and paper can give excellent results, because they provide closer personal interaction than many of the high-tech devices. And let's not forget about public websites, such as YouTube, which are free. I think the only expensive item I would suggest that parents purchase is a video editing software application, costing about $100. However, many free alternatives exist, and you may already have such an application on your computer, like Windows Live Movie Maker. My opinion is that fancy gadgets will not help you improve your daily communication with your children with autism. You need something simple, easy to use, and readily available for picture-talking with your children.

Magnetic Drawing Board

I can't begin to express my gratitude to the makers of the magnetic drawing board. It's a truly wonderful invention. Yes, I know its resolution is not particularly good and it cannot compete with modern touch-screen tablet PCs. I have also recently seen game consoles that allow people to draw pictures on big screen TVs. But, at least to me, magnetic drawing boards work better than high-tech alternatives because these low-tech drawing boards are kid-tough and do not require batteries or power cords. Also, the pen is tightly attached to the board, so you can't lose it.

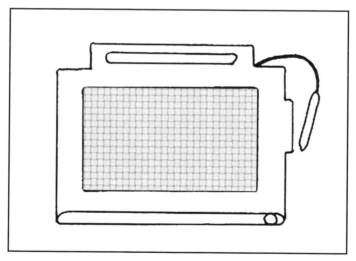

Magnetic Drawing Board

I used a magnetic drawing board as my main communication device with Mindy. Mindy learned so much from it: from alphabets to full sentences, from nice behaviors to how to detect dangerous situations. She learned about people's emotions and how to draw her own pictures, too. I used the magnetic drawing board to talk to her about her school activities, her friends, and what we were going to do the next day. We worked together to make up a story about a boy and a girl flying on a hot air balloon over a volcano, jumping out in parachutes, and being chased by a triceratops. I didn't even know that I could draw a triceratops!

Magnetic drawing boards come in several sizes. I found that the lap-sized board was the best choice. The drawing area is about the size of a typical sheet of printer paper (8.5 in. by 11 in.). It's a little big for carrying around, but you will appreciate the larger drawing area. In my opinion, the simpler the board, the better. Additional decorations around the board are unnecessary, as they will become a nuisance when you use the board day after day. These drawing boards can be found at your local urban stores (such as Target or Walmart) or toy stores. They can also be purchased online. They are sold under various names, such as magnetic doodle board, Magna Doodle, magnetic sketcher, etc.

Another option is to use whiteboards with dry erase markers. But magnetic drawing boards are better because you don't need to go look for the markers, and you don't need to worry about your kids writing on their clothes or on the wall.

Mindy learned to read from the magnetic drawing board, and she got really good at minuscule details. She familiarized herself with all the punctuation marks, and sometimes when I forgot to place punctuation marks, she would correct me and add them herself. Other times when my cartoon characters' emotions did not look quite right (like when someone should have looked surprised or worried), she would correct me by changing the shape of the character's mouth.

The following story, about the adventures of a boy and a girl, was one I made up with contributions from Mindy, using the magnetic drawing board, when Mindy was almost four years old. This story is a concrete example of the type of "picture-aided conversation" that I usually had with Mindy. I told her stories and at the same time drew pictures on the board. Communicating with pictures may seem unreal or too difficult to many people—my own parents drew a blank in their minds whenever I asked them to draw pictures for Mindy.

However, this was the way Mindy and I, pro-picture people, communicated. Initially, my wife also had trouble coming up with pictures, but she got a lot better as time went by.

The Adventures of a Boy and a Girl

	Once upon a time, there was a boy and a girl. And one day they went up flying in a hot-air balloon. They were having a lot of fun.
	But suddenly they realized that there was a volcano erupting in the distance, and they were getting closer and closer! The volcano was spewing hot lava, and had a lot of fire and a lot of smoke. The boy said, "Oh no!" and the girl said, "Jump!"
	Luckily they had two parachutes. They opened their parachutes and went down slowly.
	Little did they know that there was a triceratops waiting for them on the ground! When they saw the triceratops, the girl said, "Oh no!" and the boy said, "Run!"

	They reached a cliff by the ocean, and they jumped into the water. The triceratops could not jump. So the boy and the girl were safe...or so they thought.
	They were swimming in the water, and they saw a little fish and a little crab. But wait! What was that? There was also a big bad shark in the water. The boy said, "Oh no!" and the girl said, "Swim!"
	They hopped on dry land, but the shark kept chasing them, and it jumped out of the water, too! The poor shark hit its nose on a basketball backboard and had an owie.
	The boy and the girl found two skateboards on top of a hill, so they hopped on the skateboards and went down the slope. Weeeee!
	And that was how they got home. Mom and Dad were waiting for them outside. It was just in time for dinner, and everybody was happy.

THE END |

YouTube

In our family, I am the one who is good at solving problems with incomplete information. Once, just after moving to a new city, we were out driving around dinner time, and my wife decided where we should go for dinner. She said, "I know a good Japanese restaurant. Its name starts with the letter *O* and it's located in a mall." Back then there were no smartphones, and I was driving. We were new to town. I did not even know where the malls were. My wife had been to the restaurant with my brother-in-law once, but I had never been there. I grumbled and complained to my wife, "Why do you always make these impossible requests of me?" To make a long story short, I arrived at the restaurant within fifteen minutes. *Onami* was the name of the restaurant, and yes, it was located in a mall. "Serendipity" is the word that comes to my mind whenever we recall this happy episode in our life.

Mindy started to watch YouTube video clips early on. When she was three and half years old, one day she told me: "Papa, I want Svinka Peppa." I couldn't understand what she was saying at all. I thought she misspoke, but she was very consistent in her pronunciation. I asked my wife whether she knew anything about "Shinka Bebba." She said she had no idea. I asked Mindy what "Shinka Bebba" was, but she couldn't tell me. She was barely talking then. Later my wife told me that she remembered Mindy had recently watched a pig cartoon. I searched online until I finally hit with Peppa Pig. But that still did not explain the "Shinka" part. Mindy liked the Peppa Pig video clip that I played for her, but that was not really the one she was looking for. Then I saw one of the videos on the side panel had some Cyrillic writing in the description: Свинка Пеппа. I tried to read the Cyrillic letters, and sure enough, they spelled "Svinka Peppa." So I finally found the video clip that Mindy wanted. Mindy was watching cartoons in Russian, and we had no idea. Was I supposed to understand Mindy's Russian, too? Oh boy.

That's the kind of detective work I often do at home and at work. I work with numeric data, day in and day out. I often compare the data I work with to my children. Like my children, data is also silent.

Neither my data nor my children talk, but they all have stories to tell. If we persevere, we can discover their stories.

I am very grateful for online video clip sites such as YouTube. They contain a trove of video collections, from songs, to cartoons, to documentaries. Let me describe one particular instance where YouTube helped my children adapt to something new. Right before Mindy and Ivan's first trip by airplane, I showed them some videos. They got acquainted with the outside of an airplane, also the inside passenger cabin. By the time they got on the actual airplane, they were already familiar with it and they handled the long flight pretty well. I also used YouTube to develop Mindy's knowledge and interests. I showed her things like volcanoes with hot lava, flying blimps, the launch of Apollo rocket missions, and the moon landing. Mindy learned the names of many dinosaurs and also many songs from YouTube, which she liked to sing around the house. I don't know how my wife found so many kinds of good video clips. Many of them are educational and well suited to children with autism. Some video clips are developed for teaching English to nonnative English speakers (one example is ELF Learning, please check out their URL at http://elflearning.jp/), but they do such a good job with cartoon drawings that the video clips worked out perfectly for Mindy and Ivan. For instance, one video clip showed the emotions of various people. When Ivan used words such as "excited" and "surprised" in front of his ABA therapists, they were gladly excited and surprised.

I know parents may have concerns about children watching videos on computers. It's certainly not a good thing for their eyes. In this regard, tablet PCs and smartphones can't be any better. So use as big a screen as possible. Hooking up your TV to on-line video is a realistic choice, and there are many ways to do this. Google's Chromecast is one of these alternatives. Parents should also limit the viewing duration as well. But, as a general rule, please do not avoid technology. Children with autism need all available channels of communication. For instance, Mindy learned to send text messages to me using my wife's smartphone, when she was still five years old. Some nonverbal people with autism communicate through typing. It is always better to discover these channels of communication earlier rather than later.

Video Editing Software

All children with autism are visual. This is almost by definition: children with autism are not good at verbal communication, so they rely on their visual capability by default. Even in the case of those children with autism without speech problems, they still have strong visual inclination. I did not think verbally until my late teens. I did not have speech delay issues, but I did my thinking in pictures.

Going one level deeper, I can clearly distinguish two different groups of children with autism: the picture-memory group, and the video-memory group. Let's call the first group *pro-picture* children, and the second group *pro-video* children.

> **pro-picture** = picture-memory children
> **pro-video** = video-memory children

I consider the use of video editing software vital to the development of pro-video children. If you are willing to go through the trouble of obtaining ABA services for your child with autism, then you really should consider procuring video editing software and learning how to use it.

The technology of video editing changes very quickly. Tablet PCs are now in vogue but I am still stuck in the desktop software world. The Microsoft Windows operating system often includes Movie Maker software. I have used Movie Maker, but its features are somewhat limited. As for popular commercial video editing software, I have used both Sony Vegas and Pinnacle Studio. Perform a Google search for video editing software reviews before making a purchase, since the technology changes so quickly. I have been told that tablet PCs now also offer excellent animation software.

One important note about video clip content: This book is about how to communicate with your children visually, not about the technological details, or about third-party multimedia content. Please check applicable copyright regulations whenever you access third-party content.

One of the early video clips that I made for Mindy was a story about "Baby and Baba." It came from a game that I played with Mindy when she still did not call me Papa. I racked my brain to come up with a way to teach her to say "Papa." I thought that a sheep's bleat "bah...bah..." sounded close enough to "Papa," so I made up a story about the adventures of a baby with a big blue whale and some sheep. Anyway, Mindy did not learn to call me Papa that way, but she had fun with the story. The first time she swam in the ocean, she got so excited and came over and told me, "Daddy, I swimmed in the ocean, but I did not see the big blue whale!" It made all my efforts worth it. Curiously enough, I think the same video clip did contribute to helping Ivan call me Papa, though another video I made (the Papaosaurus video) was the main success story. The story is below, along with the images used to make the video clip. I changed the pronoun from "she" to "he" when Ivan became the primary audience for the clip.

The Story of Baby and Baba

Once upon a time, there was a little baby. She liked to go to the ocean and swim in the water. One day, she went to the beach, and jumped into the water, and started to swim like this: sweesh-sweesh, sweesh-sweesh. In the distance, she saw a big blue whale. The baby climbed on top of the big blue whale, and sat on the blowhole of the big blue whale. At that moment, the big blue whale sneezed like this: Ah-tshoo! And the baby was launched into the sky. The baby landed on a piece of white cloud, and drifted like this: tshoom-tshoom-tshoom, tshoom-tshoom-tshoom. In the distance, the baby saw a tall mountain peak. The baby hopped onto the tall mountain peak and slid down the mountain slope like this: tshoooom...tshoooom...The baby landed on a piece of green prairie, and there was a big group of sheep. The sheep said: "bah-bah, bah-bah." What did the sheep say? "Bah-bah, bah-bah." At that moment, the baby called out: "Baba, Baba." And Baba came and rescued the baby and took the baby home. THE END.

The Story of Baby and Baba

There are more advanced animation software tools, such as Adobe Director (with a hefty price tag), or free but simpler alternatives such as Pencil. If you are familiar with such tools, by all means use them. These tools are much more difficult to use. They are professional-grade multimedia tools, and they probably make more sense if you have a larger group of children with autism.

In lieu of animation tools, I often did the following four things:

- Modulate frames of static drawings into existing video clips. Most video editing applications allow you to mix picture files with video clips.
- Make video clips entirely out of frames of static drawings.
- Take photo sequences. You will need a tripod for this purpose to immobilize your camera. You can then either draw pictures on a whiteboard frame by frame, or take pictures of toys frame by frame to make them look like they are animated. I have made photo sequences that, for

example, spell out words letter by letter, or that animate a school bus moving on a toy track.

- Make a boomerang-style edit of a storyboard: Draw the picture of an entire story first, and then gradually delete elements in reverse-time sequence. The figure below shows an example. The last frame (frame #9) is drawn first. Then you remove elements after elements to generate frames #8, #7, …until you are left with the elements for frame #1. And then you make a video in the forward time sequence using frames #1, #2, …, and #9.

Example of boomerang-style edited story frames

Don't forget to add some music for your sound track, and record your own voiceover narration, too. Home video creation is fun. It is time-consuming, but your children will be able to watch your video clips over and over again. It will be well worth your time.

4x6 Index Cards and Photo Albums

Children with autism truly appreciate it when you make a personalized effort to communicate with them, in their language. This is especially so with Ivan. By the age of three, he could already understand my picture drawings. Sometimes I drew pictures for him on paper napkins when we went out to restaurants for dinner. And he would hold on to the paper napkins as if they were something important.

Magnetic drawing boards are great for real-time picture talking. But for more permanent drawings, I used 4x6 index cards and mini photo albums of the same size. I made personalized card albums for both Mindy and Ivan. Both of them loved their personalized card albums. And it was truly heartwarming to see Ivan picking up some of his old card albums and flipping through them from time to time. Children can feel your love for them through those silly simple drawings.

The 4x6 index cards I used can be found in office supply stores or art supply stores. Blank cards are much better for drawing purposes than ruled cards, but they are harder to find. You can order them online if you can't find blank index cards in your local stores.

These index cards fit perfectly in 4x6 photo albums. These albums can be purchased online or in urban stores (e.g., Target or Walmart) for a dollar or two. There are two styles of photo albums: side-loading and top-loading. The top-loading version is more child-proof but harder to handle: it is harder to slip the index cards into the plastic pouches, as well as to remove them. So unless your children are really young and/or mischievous, I would recommend the side-loading version. Your children may rip apart these albums at the beginning, but they will grow out of this bad habit with time, and your card albums will survive longer and longer.

As for pens, any pen will do. Ballpoint pens are safer since the ink is less likely to get on your clothing, or on your other important papers, but permanent, fine-point markers may look neater. You'll have to make a judgment call as to which is more suitable for you.

I don't attach much sentimental value to the drawings. The index cards and albums are cheap, so I use them as "consumable" devices. I assembled card albums for topics that I believe the children need to look at repeatedly. For instance, I use a card album for my children's daily routine schedule (waking up, having breakfast, going to school, having dinner, going to sleep, etc.). In Ivan's case, due to his fascination with the vacuum cleaner and our desire to participate with him, I also made a card album for his activities related to the vacuum cleaner. Vocabulary acquisition and simple two-way conversations can also be drawn on index cards. Just like video clips, the good thing about card albums is that you can show them over and over again to your children, day after day. And children can also use the albums to indicate their needs, when they are still non-verbal.

Picture Journal

The lives of normal children are so much easier. As soon as they start to talk, they have completed an **outer feedback loop**. They can hear their own voices and start to perform complex reasoning. For children with autism, this oral-aural feedback loop is simply not there. Children with autism are visual. In order for them to complete their outer feedback loops, they need to be able to generate their own manual-visual outputs. For pro-picture children, that means writing and drawing. Until they can write and draw in their own picture journals, pro-picture children are at a disadvantage with respect to their typical peers because they haven't closed their outer feedback loop yet. As for pro-video children, they should also be encouraged to write and draw, after they are capable of these skills. Prior to that, building block toys may offer an easier place to start their manual-visual feedback loop.

That is, emphasis should be placed on developing drawing and writing skills of children with autism. Once they are able close their outer feedback loops, they will be able to develop deep reasoning skills to help them catch up and perhaps even overtake their typical peers. Encourage your children to keep picture journals, where they can work on developing their imaginations. Please note that not all journal notebooks are alike. Because children with autism are visual, it's best to have journal notebooks that come with reserved space for drawing pictures.

Pro-video children tend to be less patient with picture journal writing; their natural language is video clips, not static picture journals. Until video creation software becomes more child user friendly to allow them to make video journals, it is important to encourage pro-video children to keep a picture journal consistently. This will help them develop their speech skills as well as more complex reasoning skills.

Picture journals are harder to find. I recommend several kinds: Mead brand's "Primary Journal," and Lakeshore brand's "My First Writing Prompts Journal," "My First Draw & Write Journal," and "Draw & Write Journal." Check them out and see which best suits your child.

Paper Signs and Masking Tape

Masking tape is the type of tape you use in a paint job, so that you can mask off areas that you don't want to paint. One property of painter's masking tape is that it won't damage wall surfaces. It's usually very easy to remove and it also does not leave sticky residue. The purpose of using painter's masking tape is to mount index cards, paper sheets, and paper signs on the wall or other vertical surfaces. I use it in place of double-sided mounting tape. I tear off a length of masking tape and roll it into a small-size ribbon ring, with the sticky side on the outside. I then use these ribbon rings as makeshift mounting tape, and place little cards or paper sheets with drawings or words all over the house. This way I can teach my children new words and sentences. If you want something sturdier than paper sheets or index cards, you can also cut out a small piece of white foam board. I prefer foam boards that are 3/16 inches thick and are covered with glossy paper. I draw tiny pictures and write some words, cut the board into a small sign, and then tape the back with masking tape rings. This way, the children could detach the sign from the wall and reattach it elsewhere. Those mini signs themselves are a good toy for the children, almost like puzzle pieces.

Document Scanner and Digital Drawing Tablet

For video editing, a document scanner makes drawing easier. You can draw by hand on paper and scan the image into your computer, then use image editing software to do some post-capture cleaning. You can get cheap flatbed or portable scanners for around $50, and many printers also come with scanner capability (known as "all-in-one"). I also used a digital drawing tablet which allowed me to draw pictures directly into a computer. With today's touchscreen computers and tablet PCs, there are newer and better alternatives for drawing pictures directly onto your computer.

Once the pictures/drawings are scanned into the computer, you can clean up or edit the images a little bit. Most computers come with some basic image editing programs (e.g., Microsoft Paint, Microsoft Photo Editor). Camera and scanner vendors usually include photo-editing software with their devices. Some websites offer free online image editing applications, such as Sumopaint. GIMP is a more advanced graphics editor, with many powerful features. Google around to find options that suit your needs and budget.

Cheap Digital Camera and Tripod

If you do decide to invest in a camera, I recommend getting a cheap one. For $30 or so, you can get an OK camera that shoots both pictures and video clips. Also get a tripod so you can immobilize your camera for more stable shooting. Some of these cheap cameras come with an integrated USB plug, which makes the file transfer process from camera to computer or TV easier. I don't find it worthwhile to invest in expensive cameras, since the transferring of contents can be difficult and, as a result, you may use the camera less often. Also, as it has happened to me, your children may be over-enthusiastic in helping you with taking pictures and video, which is great fun to them, but could abruptly spell the end of your camera. Gadgets just don't survive long in the hands of children. Today's smartphones come with great camera features, but the same caveat applies. It suffices to say that I have also lost one smartphone to my children.

I don't find straight family video shots from cameras very educational. I suggest creating hand-drawn content on a whiteboard, and then capturing it with your camera. Using video editing software, you control the voice-over (sound track) much better, and you can arrange your cartoon drawings to convey educational messages. Nice sound tracks also attract your child's attention. As a person with autism, I remember I preferred simple cartoon images much more than real-life video clips. I have talked to other adults with autism, and it seems like from both the pro-video camp and from the pro-picture camp, the consensus is that people with autism prefer simplicity in video. We like cartoon video clips much more than real-life video shots. It is a more effective way to convey focused messages to your children so that they can learn.

I used a camera to capture the faces of family members, and to teach my children to recognize their relatives and their names that way. Cameras can also be used to capture repetitive behaviors of children with autism, also known as "stims," standing for "self-stimulation" processes. My suggestion is to modulate the children's stimming behaviors into some of their favorite video clips. The children can benefit from watching their own behaviors from the outside, so that they can connect their inner world with the outside world. You can use the stimming pictures or videos to establish a schedule, too, such as, "first do this" and "then stim."

Tablet PCs and Smartphones

I am sure in the near future tablet PCs and smartphones will offer a great platform for video capturing and editing. They may also offer a good platform for hand drawing. But as of mid-2013, I think this sector is still a bit immature. Despite the immaturity, tablet programs like finger painting could be fun for children with autism. Mindy enjoys doodling with finger painting programs on smart phones and tablet PCs. Older children may prefer drawing with a stylus.

There are also apps available for tablets and smartphones at the website for the organization Autism Speaks (please visit their site at http://www.autismspeaks.org/). Despite the wide availability of apps, it is still vital that you interact with your children to help them learn their daily routines and how to handle typical situations. Each family has some very specific needs that software developers cannot possibly foresee. Let's be frank: a parent cannot be replaced by a computer.

Books

While there are not a lot of comic books out there suitable for children with autism, Bill Watterson's *Calvin and Hobbes* and Charles M. Schulz's *Peanuts* are two good options. The vocabulary in these comic books, though geared towards adults, overlaps well with children's speech, and the speech bubbles and letter styles of these series are more readable than other comic books. Bill Watterson, in particular, deserves credit because he manages to entertain adults while preserving a child's perspective. Some parents may not like Bill Watterson's mischievous character Calvin. My wife was alarmed when Mindy started to complain and scream like Calvin. But to me, it's a good thing that the children can verbalize their feelings, even if it means shouting and screaming a little bit.

For younger children, early reading material can include Bob Books, an early reader series that is available in hard copy and digital app form, and Dr. Seuss books for young readers. Dr. Seuss worked pretty well with Mindy, while Ivan preferred the simpler Bob Books.

For older children, the *Diary of a Wimpy Kid* series, written and illustrated by Jeff Kinney, is great because it is written from a first-person perspective, and it has more template sentences that children can borrow and use. Moreover, it's one of the few books that is sprinkled with cartoon drawings that children with autism can appreciate. There is a similar series geared toward girls called *Dork Diaries*, by Rachel Renee Russell, but I find its personality and language out of sync with the style of children with autism. A similar series geared toward boys is the *Big Nate* series, by Lincoln Peirce. The font style of this series is more comfortable to read than *Diary of a Wimpy Kid*. However, as far as first-person perspective goes, I like *Diary of the Wimpy Kid* better. The *Junie B. Jones* series, by Barbara Park, is particularly great for little girls, but has fewer drawings. By age five,

Mindy started to enjoy third-person perspective books like the *Ivy and Bean* series, by Annie Barrow.

Mindy's understanding of a character's emotion was just uncanny. She could perfectly recognize a character's feelings from the drawings and from the letter styles. As she was reading *Calvin and Hobbes*, when it was Calvin's mom's turn to speak, Mindy would use a gentle and motherly tone, but when Calvin spoke, she would switch to a screaming voice. She also liked all the sound-effect words, words like "PLOOIE!" "GRONK!" "ARGH!" "EEP!" "BANG," and "BOING." I think comic books really helped her with learning to verbalize her emotions.

Digital Voice Recorder

I consider a digital voice recorder to be optional for a variety of reasons. First, I have not been able to find a digital voice recorder that is simple enough. Most come with too many buttons and too many features that I don't need. Second, unlike a cell phone, if you misplace your voice recorder, you will have a hard time finding it. Third, children tend to look at it as a gadget, and you will have to struggle to get it back from them. Fourth, voice recorders are not very cheap. (You can get a decent one for about $35.) They can be ruined easily in the hands of your child, or when you leave them exposed to too much sunlight/heat.

Still, digital voice recorders can come in handy. Although most smartphones have applications to record voice memos, the number of taps required to activate these applications makes them impractical. Some digital voice recorders can be set up so you only need to press one or two buttons to start recording. The battery-saving feature is getting better, so digital voice recorders can be used for a while before you need to change the batteries. I have used digital voice recorders for three purposes:

- As a personal digital assistant (PDA) to keep track of my daily to-do items.
- As a way to teach my children sentences. Usually I use it in conjunction with a picture drawn on paper or on a magnetic

drawing board. This is a quick-and-dirty substitute for video clips.

- As a way to capture my children's voices. I play their voices into the microphone of my laptop, and use the recordings for voice-over narration in video clips. Children love it when they recognize their own voices in the video clips. Sure, the sound quality recorded this way is horrible, but that is OK. Our aim is not to create professional-grade multimedia titles—we only need the bare minimum sound quality for our homemade video clips.

All in all, a digital voice recorder is a good gadget to have, but it has not been essential in the development of my children.

Final Words on Materials

I can't stress this point enough: go cheap. Each child with autism is different, so some of the materials/toys may work, and some may not. It's a long process to figure out which tools work best for your child. Therefore, be budget conscious in your purchases because you may find that some of your purchases may go to waste in this process.

3

PRO-VIDEO CHILDREN

Two Types of Autism: Pro-picture and Pro-video

From my personal experience interacting with children and adults with autism, I have noticed two distinct groups of people: one group relying mainly on their picture memory, and another group relying mainly on their video memory. I call them **pro-picture** people and **pro-video** people, respectively. As for the relative prevalence of these two groups, my personal observation tells me they are equally prevalent: about half of the people with autism are pro-picture and the other half are pro-video.

My daughter Mindy, my nephew Pi, and I fall into the pro-picture group, whereas my son Ivan, my nephew Tin, and my brother-in-law Pham fall into the pro-video group. Pro-picture children like to look at pictures; they tend to be more on the quiet side. They are good at phonics and they may start reading early. On the opposite side, pro-video children cannot stand looking at static pictures. They are not good at phonics or at reading. They tend to slur their speech. They are often described as hyperactive or having attention deficit disorder, labels that are misleading because these children can focus very well when doing activities that they like. Since autism is on a spectrum of manifestations, I wouldn't be surprised to find children that exhibit a mixture of behaviors from these two groups. Also, I wouldn't be surprised if some children with autism don't fall into either group. But from all cases of children with autism that I have seen directly or indirectly, I would venture to say that this classification is not only generally applicable, but it can also help parents choose appropriate techniques to communicate with their children, no matter where their children fall on the spectrum.

These two groups of children store information differently in their brains, which reminds me of something I learned from my calculus and modern physics classes. The way pro-picture children store information, versus the way pro-video children store information, is like storing information in the coordinate space versus in the momentum space. The two schemes are the *Fourier transforms* of each other, also known as *conjugates*. The fundamental memory units for pro-picture children are static images or concepts. The fundamental memory units for pro-video children are dynamic videos or processes.

I will attempt to explain Fourier transforms by using an adjective-noun analogy. In a sense, adjectives and nouns can be thought of as Fourier transforms of each other. Suppose we are attempting to describe the adjective *red* by using only nouns, then we might resort to words such as *apple, blood, strawberry, lips, tomato*, etc. Or if we are attempting to describe the noun *lemon* by using only adjectives, we might resort to words such as *juicy, sour, yellow, round, edible*, etc. That is, an adjective touches upon many nouns, and conversely, a noun touches upon many adjectives. Given sufficient numbers of words, we can infer a noun from a set of adjectives, or an adjective from a set of nouns. What's simple in one dimension (one single adjective or one single noun), becomes complex to describe in the other dimension (many nouns or many adjectives). Believe it or not, this simplicity-complexity duality has a name: it's known in science as "Heisenberg's uncertainty principle." A localized signal in one space (known as "Dirac delta") would translate into a broadly distributed signal in the other space, known as "white noise." Strictly speaking, "white noise" is random; whereas Dirac delta's Fourier transform is deterministic. But since we are not doing mathematics here, we will abuse the terminology a little bit.

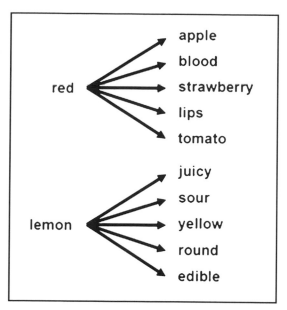

Describing an adjective by using nouns, or describing a noun by using adjectives. A simple word in one space turns into something complex in the other space.

This helps to explain why pro-video children can't stand looking at static pictures or dealing with isolated concepts. To these children, what's meaningful to us is instead perceived as noise to them.

Similarly, on a different visual-verbal plane, both groups of children with autism are visual, and our verbal commands may come across to them as white noise. The situation is worse for pro-video children, since they additionally perceive static images also as white noise.

Pro-video children have a tougher time understanding isolated concepts. Parents and teachers of pro-video children may try very hard to teach their children concepts as simple as saying the words "Mom" and "Dad." These tasks are not always as simple as they seem, and both adults and children often become frustrated. Similarly, we may try to make the children focus their eyes on specific objects, and they just look elsewhere, appearing totally noncompliant. It's not the fault of pro-video children—our signals are coming across to them as white noise!

To help you understand how a child with autism might feel, hearing all of our signals as white noise, let me tell you a story about my wife. My parents speak the Taiwanese variety of a Chinese dialect known as Minnan. When my parents came to visit us, they would stay for several weeks at a time. My wife usually communicated with my parents through a combination of hand gestures plus some broken Spanish. Usually, about one or two weeks into my parents' visit, my wife would find some excuse to go visit her own parents for a day or two. I never paid much attention to it. But one time she finally told me the truth: she couldn't stand listening to a language that she didn't understand for too many days, and she needed to take a break. She liked to get "detoxed," I guess. I told her, "Hey, that's not fair, what about me listening to your parents' Vietnamese, day in and day out?" I never complained, even though at times I felt the same way! My wife just smiled at me and said: "Yes, I know. I don't know how you manage it, but I really appreciate it."

The truth is, deep down I understood my wife. I knew some basic Vietnamese because I took a few courses. But in her case, the size of her Taiwanese vocabulary is limited to a few words here and there. So it was unfair to compare her situation with my situation. Nonetheless, it all goes to show that when we are bombarded with signals that we don't understand, we can get exhausted and frustrated. That is true even for a normal, non-autistic adult. Now, imagine that you are a child with autism and your parents keep bombarding you with white noise. How would that make you feel?

Crystal Children and Indigo Children

I remember watching an astronomy professor from my college days being interviewed by a TV reporter once, right after the New Year. The TV reporter asked the professor to forecast what was to come that year and provide the TV audience with some advice. Startled, the professor tried to deflect the question as best as he could. The TV reporter persisted with the same question again, and one could see that the professor was feeling really uncomfortable, but he politely declined one more time. Good heavens. The reporter was obviously mixing up astronomy with astrology!

Now, I am a scientist and I am not into astrology, palm reading, or card reading, so don't ask me to do any of those. I prefer astronomy, and the use of science to understand the sky and space. That being said, after I started to write this book, my brother told my parents that I was a crystal child. The terms "crystal children" and "indigo children" come from the New Age spiritual movement. My mom related to me what my brother told her. However, her words were in a different language, and translated into English it was more like "crystal man." So I did not hit on the right keywords, and did not pay attention to this term for the longest time. Only when my sister forwarded me an article on crystal children did I finally understand what it was all about.

I frankly admire the findings of these New Age specialists on this particular subject. They clearly detected two types of issues in early child development, and they labeled these two types as "crystal children" and "indigo children." (Well, there is also a third type labeled as "rainbow children," but I couldn't make sense out of this latter group.) I found that I could map these two types of children into my own explanation of the two types of autism:

> Crystal children → Pro-picture
> Indigo children → Pro-video

Basically, what drove me to establish this parallel is that the crystal child is described as quiet, empathic, etc., whereas the indigo child is described as hyperactive. Another aspect where I agree with the New Age movement is in their belief that these children are born with special missions. They are here to tell us something.

I'll stop here before I dive further into the mystical realm. I am not here to promote spiritualism. Like my astronomy professor, I get uncomfortable when I get into these issues. But I give credit to the New Age specialists for observing the existence of these two special groups of children.

Pro-video Children and Focus on Processes

Pro-video children focus on processes, not on isolated objects, images, or concepts. This reminds me of another analogy from software programming. Some of you may have heard about "object-oriented programming." (Some programmers like to call it the "object-oriented programming system," so they can use the funny acronym OOPS.) Well, if pro-picture children follow the "object-oriented programming" paradigm, then pro-video children follow the "aspect-oriented programming" paradigm. In the first paradigm, program code is factored in a vertical fashion, whereas in the second paradigm, program code is factored in a horizontal direction. Whereas pro-picture children focus on objects/concepts, pro-video children focus on aspects/processes.

In order to understand the difference between pro-video and pro-picture children, I developed a mental picture of human brain's wiring. So let me describe my understanding of the visual memory part of the human brain, by using the diagram below as a guide.

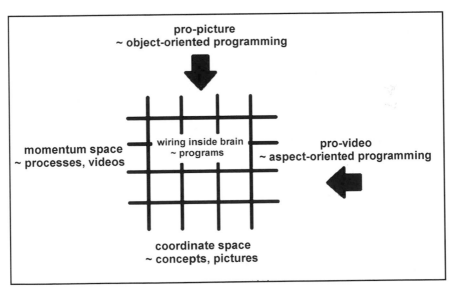

Brain wiring: pro-video vs. pro-picture

We likely have a "memory grid" that is capable of storing both concepts and processes. As a convention, let us lay the concept dimension on the horizontal axis and the process dimension on the vertical axis. When we perform our thinking process, our brain signals travel over this memory grid in a zigzag pattern, like a cab driver in Manhattan or a mouse in a maze. And from time to time our brains reprogram themselves by rewiring the connections.

Different children learn things differently. To me, pro-picture children tend to learn things "vertically," and pro-video children tend to learn things "horizontally." That is, they navigate their taxi cabs in Brain City's streets differently. One day both groups of children will end up learning everything they need to learn, but their paths traveled will be different.

As a pro-picture person, I find that communicating with pro-video children is a tougher challenge. To deal with a pro-video child like my son Ivan, I had no textbooks to follow, and my instincts were often off the mark, so it took me a lot of time and effort to come up with solutions. However, nothing is more rewarding than when your children realize that you are finally speaking their language—that you are finally communicating with them.

To communicate with pro-video children, the first thing to remember is that they like videos, not static pictures. I guess that's part of the challenge of autism special education: in the past, making videos was not a practical option. Today, with modern computer devices and software, video editing is no longer a privilege of specialists. Home video editing has become very popular. So if at all possible, I would advise parents to acquire some basic video editing skills. True, there are tons of educational videos and games out there, but they won't address the very specific needs of all children with autism and their families. Moreover, those third-party videos and games will be missing a personal touch and won't help you develop your relationship with your children. Let's look at it this way: your children are trying very hard to speak *your* language, but have you ever really tried to speak *their* language? We are not talking about becoming video-editing professionals; we are talking about making the crudest/silliest video clips so that you can communicate simple messages to your children. These messages can be as simple as helping your children learn to call you "Mom" or "Dad."

The second thing to remember about pro-video children is that they store information about processes in their memory, not objects. They may appear to be passionate or obsessive about certain objects, but in reality they are not after the objects. What they are really after is the whole process of getting the object and playing with it. The objects themselves are not the ultimate driver—the process is.

The Amazing "Fractal" Brain

My wife comes from a big family, and once in a while we all go on a vacation together. During one such family trip, everyone grilled our brother-in-law Pham, who is a pro-video person, about how pro-video people actually store information inside their brains. I always felt like I just did not understand the memory structure of pro-video people. Their brains were clearly different from mine. So I asked Pham: "How do you store information inside your brain?" As a point of comparison, I told him that inside my brain, I stored things in images, like a picture album or comic strip.

What he described to me was very interesting. First of all, he said that he did not store information the way I did. He remembers things as a string of events or activities. This confirmed my conjecture about pro-video people storing processes instead of isolated concepts or images. However, what he told me next left me shocked and in awe. He said he memorizes things in levels. He has a gross sequence of events at the top level. When he recalls a sequence of events, he can focus at any particular spot, and then "zoom in" at that spot for more details. Not only that, he can successively "zoom in" to focus at finer and finer details. I dropped my jaw at his description. For the first time I realized just how beautiful the pro-video mind was. No wonder some of these people can recall details with uncanny precision. Their brains are not distracted by unnecessary thoughts, so they can focus and zoom in, and zoom in, and zoom in, until they retrieve all the details. "Fractal" was the term that came to mind.

This is not a book about mathematics. And I did not write this book to explain "fractals" or "self-similarities" at length. I will just say that "fractals" are mathematical constructions that explain shapes like tree branches, snow flakes, and other recursive-repetitive patterns, where the finer and finer details resemble the broader/overall structure as you "zoom in." If you are curious about fractals, you can read about them on Wikipedia. I will just limit myself here to sharing a picture taken from Wikipedia on the most famous fractal set: the Mandelbrot set. (This image is reproduced under public domain license permission from Wikipedia.) I think without explaining the details, it is clear from the picture that the "cardioid" or heart-like shape of the structure repeats itself at finer and finer levels of the image, *ad infinitum.*

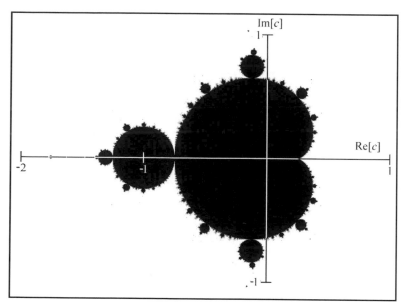

A famous example of a fractal: the Mandelbrot set

I feel so sad that the beautiful and powerful minds of the pro-video people are so misunderstood in our society. In the past, these people were sent to mental institutions—what a waste of their talents. Today, they are still not understood by our society. We keep forcing them to adapt to our status quo; we keep forcing them to socialize like typical children. We place the entire burden of communication on them because we do not truly understand where their strengths lie. We don't let them develop in a way that is natural to them. We just keep bombarding them with white noise, day after day, week after week, and year after year. My hope is that in the near future we can change our society's attitude, and provide pro-video children with a development program that best suits their natural growth path.

Video Clips to Teach Echoing and Verbalizing

Pro-video children absorb information much more readily through video clips. Therefore, if you want them to learn to verbalize and answer questions, by all means prepare some video clips. The video clips don't need to be fancy. For conversation-style communication, you don't even need to put in a music sound track. Your video clips can help you address specific concerns in your daily interaction with your children.

Here is an example of a video clip I prepared for Ivan for something very simple: voice-tone exercise and speech-bubble familiarization. When Ivan was age three, he always spoke in a robotic voice. I got used to communicating with him in his peculiar robotic voice, but one day I thought I should introduce him to a normal person's tone of voice. Also, I wanted to start to familiarize him with speech bubbles, so he could develop his reading skills. So I made a video with only a few frames. In the image frames below, the text in the right column represents the voice-over narration used in each frame. All the voice-overs are done with my voice, but I imitated Ivan's robotic voice in most frames. "Honey bear" is a toy I made from a commercial honey container. I punched a small hole at the bottom of the plastic bear-shaped container. The original idea was to give my children a visual aid for potty training, but that did not work out well in practice. Still, the honey bear became a good bathroom toy for both Mindy and Ivan. They would squeeze the honey bear and it would go pee-pee. So it was a lot of fun for the children.

I played the video clip for Ivan over and over again before giving him a bath. When bath time came, I followed the frame sequence exactly up to the point of asking him: "Was it fun?" and he replied, "Yes, it was fun!" with a non-robotic voice. Mission accomplished.

Video clip to practice tone of voice and familiarize Ivan with speech bubbles

YES, IT WAS FUN!	*(Normal voice)* Yes, it was fun!
TAKE A BATH HONEY BEAR GOES PEE PEE.	*(Ivan's signature robotic voice)* Take a bath. Honey bear goes pee-pee.
ALL DONE!	*(Ivan's signature robotic voice)* All done!
WAS IT FUN?	*(Ivan's signature robotic voice)* Was it fun? *(Notice speech bubble from Daddy)*
WAS IT FUN? YES, IT WAS FUN!	*(Normal voice)* Yes, it was fun! *(Notice speech bubble on child)*

THE END	(*silent*)

So after this exercise Ivan learned to say perhaps his first sentence with a normal person's voice, instead of his robotic voice. He also learned to recognize speech bubbles. To a normal person, these may seem like trivial steps. But for children with autism, these are vital skills that the child's future development depends on. Being able to recognize speech bubbles meant that I could start to do picture-aided talking with him using the magnetic drawing board. Compared to video preparation, picture-aided talking methods require less time, and help children learn equally well.

I repeatedly emphasize that third-party video clips and games are no replacement for homemade video clips. Only parents are able to capture the intimate daily life of their children, and parents' voices also provide a sense of familiarity that cannot be achieved by any other person's voice. Your voice will catch the attention of your children so powerfully. With my first few videos, Ivan and Mindy were surprised to hear my voice coming out of the computer or TV set. It was like, Daddy, you are over here, but how come your voice is coming out from the TV/computer? That in itself was a lot of fun for the children. Your daily family life is unique, and you should base your video clips on it, no matter how silly it may appear to others.

The following is a video clip I made for Ivan to teach him to say the word "No." I modulated the message into one of Mindy and Ivan's favorite daily activities: to sit on the hammock we had in our living room. Ivan used to make a nonsensical uttering that sounded like "Oi oi, ay-o-wah" and he followed that with a really cute burst of laughter. Mindy picked it up, too. So I captured and recorded their voices, and drew a cartoon representation of them sitting on the hammock. It took me about 40 minutes to make the video. I played it over and over again for Mindy and Ivan. They loved it and could watch the video forever. My wife said that those 40 minutes that I spent were totally worth it, and I agreed. Whenever I played the video, Mindy and Ivan would go sit in the hammock and repeat their uttering and laughter concurrently with the video, and I would ask Ivan the same question as in the video: "Ivan, are you a bad boy?" and Ivan would then reply in sync with the video: "No, I am a good boy!" Seriously, you cannot get better quality family time than that.

Oi, Oi, Ay-o-wah video clip

The "Oi Oi" video was so successful that it turned itself into Ivan's new addiction. That was a good thing, though, because I could modify the video clip to teach him other new skills. The next thing I did was to replace the final two frames about "bad boy/good boy" with a brand new sequence. I taught him instead how to have a telephone conversation. (We had a spare phone set at home, so we used it as a toy for Ivan.) The new frames are depicted next.

You should have seen Ivan's reaction when he first saw this modified version. One would think Ivan would be surprised or disconcerted because he was expecting the "good boy" part, which I had replaced with the phone conversation sequence. But what happened was that he immediately noticed the difference and glued his eyes to the new sequence. He gave his full attention to every single frame, despite their long duration. He watched the new video clip over and over again. That weekend my wife took the children to visit their cousins while I stayed home. I called my wife, and told her to pass the phone to Ivan. You may have already guessed the result: Ivan was able to talk to me on the phone, following the exact same sequence. It worked the very first time, and it worked like a charm. Now I could talk to Ivan on the phone—another milestone reached. And in this process, he also learned to differentiate between the questions "How old are you?" and "How are you?" which he had difficulty telling apart before. Phone skills meant another door was now open. Because the telephone is usually a very interesting device to children, you can hold their attention and start to ask them many other questions, and introduce them to extended conversation skills.

Telephone conversation frames

Pro-video children are truly pro-video clips. Once you understand this, you can teach them almost anything. Attention deficit disorder? What attention deficit disorder?

Answering Yes and No

Among the initial videos that I made for Ivan, teaching him to answer yes or no was one of the most important achievements.

Ivan was not answering yes or no questions. However, I knew two things that he absolutely disliked: hot sauce and nose rinsing (when his nose was stuffed up).

I achieved my goal of teaching him to say yes and no by making one more follow-up to the "Oi Oi" hammock video. In the video clip, after the initial "Oi Oi" part, I asked him:

Papa: "Do you like drums?"
Ivan: "Yes, I do."
Papa: "Do you like hot sauce?"
Ivan: "No, I don't."
Papa: "Do you like milk?"
Ivan: "Yes, I do."

So that video had two positive answers and one negative answer. I made another video clip with two negative answers and one positive answer:

Papa: "Do you like hot sauce?"
Ivan: "No, I don't."
Papa: "Do you like to rinse your nose?"
Ivan: "No, I don't."
Papa: "Do you like chips?"
Ivan: "Yes, I do."

And that was how Ivan learned to answer yes or no questions. I guess the teachers and therapists might have found it overly polite for Ivan to always answer with full sentences, "Yes, I do" and "No, I don't." But functionally speaking, the goal was achieved. I did not mind Ivan seeming over polite. It is better than being impolite, right?

Mouthing

At some point in Ivan's childhood, he developed a mouthing issue. He would put his mouth on just about anything: shirt sleeves, toys, the hammock, the handrail of the stairs, etc.

This issue did not need a video clip. Ivan hated hot sauce, so I recycled the idea from the hot sauce video. One day, I put some mild hot sauce on a toy that he was mouthing. He did not even need to taste the hot sauce; just looking at what I was doing was a strong enough message for him. I then asked him, "Do you like hot sauce?" To which he replied with a loud and clear, "No, I don't!" Afterwards, every time he was mouthing something, it was sufficient for me to ask him, "Do you like hot sauce?" and he would understand my message and make a conscious effort to stop. His mouthing problem gradually subsided.

Understanding the Concept of "Or"

I was an easy kid when it came to food. When my mother asked me whether I wanted an apple or an orange, my answer was always, "Either one would be fine." That drove my mom crazy. How in the world could someone have no preference? But to me, eating an apple or an orange was about the least important decision I had to make in my life. It truly did not make any difference to me. Even to this day, food is still at the very bottom of my priority list. I basically eat anything. My wife always complains that it is pointless to prepare nice meals for me. No matter how much effort she puts into making a dish, if she doesn't ask me on the spot, five minutes later I won't remember what I ate.

Ivan was pickier about food than me. Still, for dessert, Ivan was a very easygoing boy. If you offered him an apple or an orange, he would just pick the last item in your sentence. In other words, he was simply echoing, and not really making a decision. My wife pointed that out to me, and asked me whether I could do something about it.

It took me a bit of effort to teach Ivan to understand the concept of the conjunction "or." It's probably difficult for typical people to realize that children with autism need to be taught things as simple as the word "or," which most typical children learn without much effort at all.

I remembered the success of the hot sauce video, so I recycled the idea and drew some pictures on the magnetic drawing board. I asked Ivan whether he liked a banana or hot sauce, and then made sure to flip the order of hot sauce and banana from time to time. After we practiced on the drawing board, we practiced it in real life. Then I replaced banana and hot sauce with other things that he liked or disliked. Within just a few days, he mastered the concept of "or," and stopped always choosing the second item offered.

When I first observed Ivan saying "Oi Oi" in the hammock, I had no idea that later on I'd need to teach Ivan to stop mouthing, or to understand the "or" conjunction. From his hammock experience, he learned to say "Yes" and "No," and then to say "No, I don't" to hot sauce. Then from the hot sauce idea he learned to stop mouthing upon my verbal command. And then he learned to understand the "or" conjunction through my drawings, without a video clip. In each instance, I modulated a new message into a previous experience. I built one bridge after another. At the beginning Ivan needed video clip input, towards the end he understood my verbal command. That's the essence of Eikona Bridge: patching the communication gap between our children and us, the adults.

When Ivan reached age four, he was still not talking much. However, functionally he was able to make requests, follow instructions, and answer questions about preferences. Ivan also acquired good pro-picture and reading skills, meaning that I no longer needed to make video clips as often as before. Life gradually became easier for the whole family.

The Real Message behind Repetitive Behaviors

If pro-video children exhibit a repetitive behavior and are obsessed with certain objects or actions, the wrong thing to do is to try to suppress their obsession. This repetitive behavior is a fundamental entity in the momentum space, a building block in their native language. It is a way for these children to tell others, "Here is the door to my world, please come on in." And they have been trying to tell you since…forever! So please learn their language and listen to them, even though at first sight their repetitive behavior may appear to you as purposeless "white noise." We, the parents, are guilty of sending them white noise when we speak to them in our language, and we also listen to them incorrectly by interpreting their signals as white noise. We are not only impeding communication, but actually breaking it in both directions. This madness has got to stop!

In diagram below, I illustrate my understanding of repetitive behaviors by using another copy of the street map of Brain City.

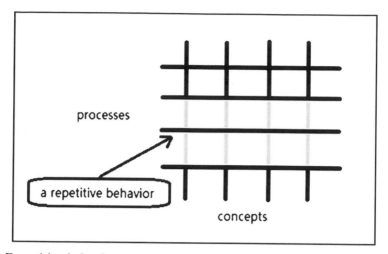

Repetitive behaviors are processes unconnected to other processes

I identify repetitive behaviors with processes unconnected (or weakly connected) to other processes. In that sense, they are isolated: they are Dirac deltas in the momentum space. They are the building blocks inside the brains of pro-video children. Repetitive behaviors are like highways running through a city: the taxi cabs cannot simply make a turn and hop onto a perpendicular street, if there is no exit ramp.

People may try very hard to understand the meaning of repetitive behaviors, but I have a different opinion. If we asked people to explain isolated concepts, such as "chair," let's see what they might answer. Merriam-Webster dictionary says: "*A seat for one person that has a back and usually four legs.*" So, to understand the concept of "chair," people need to connect it to other concepts such as "seat," "person," "back," and "legs." In other words, "chair" itself does not really have a meaning per se. It acquires meaning only when it is connected to other concepts. Similarly, repetitive behaviors are the building blocks in pro-video children's brains, but these building blocks themselves don't have much of a meaning. They will acquire meaning only after they are connected to other processes. And it's our job to provide such connections for our children. In other words, I believe it is a waste of time to go on a wild goose chase to explain the repetitive behaviors. I'd rather spend my time connecting my children's repetitive behaviors to those vital skills that they still need to learn.

If you are concerned about the diagram, and think that the lack of connections means that there is damage to the neurons, then I would say your perspective is too negative. I have a much more positive take on this. Because the building blocks in children with autism are less "pre-connected," they actually get less distracted, and have the potential to be better "programmed." Fewer initial connections do not mean fewer final connections. As a matter of fact, it means they have better concentration, and this may explain why many children with autism turn out to be geniuses when they grow up. So if you want to lament the lack of initial connections or the presence of autistic symptoms, then maybe you would like to find out about successful people with autism first. Trust me, when you want to drive your taxi cab through a megalopolis, you will appreciate the presence of a few highways. Highways without exits are useless, but with a few exits here and there, they become the backbone of transportation.

Furthermore, based on the research articles I have read, the autistic brain appears to have more connections than the typical brain. In a sense, there is no lack of connections. All the connections for verbalizing and socialization are there. It's just that due to a strong auto-feedback mechanism, the autistic brain enters a resonance mode, and prefers to revisit the same route over and over again. We will talk more about this in a later chapter, when I discuss the radio-circuit analogy.

So I view repetitive behaviors as building blocks in the pro-video brain, and I do not find anything inherently wrong with these behaviors. Matter of fact, I am endeared by these pristine signals of human brain. I know many parents and therapists would be aghast at joining their children with autism in repetitive behaviors. Let us take Ivan's fascination with the vacuum cleaner as an example. One might express concern about Ivan, thinking: What kind of skill is it to play with a vacuum cleaner all day long? Who would want their child to play with a vacuum cleaner 10 hours a day, day after day? Why not stop this pointless repetitive behavior, so that the child can have time to learn something useful instead?

Stopping the behavior seems like a good plan, right? Unfortunately, many parents with children with autism will tell you that what actually happens is that they run into tremendous problems trying to suppress their children's repetitive behaviors, and more often than not ruin their relationships with the children along the way. On top of that, they achieve little in teaching the children additional skills. The adults keep banging their heads against this brick wall and are unable to figure a way out. Sounds familiar? This is the same sad story that we hear over and over again from one autistic family to another. My question is: why do the adults artificially create a problem where there was none? Trust me, the children are fine. The adults are the ones who have created the problem! The children's behaviors don't need to change—the adults' behaviors do!

Modulation: You Can Move the Earth

Archimedes, the ancient Greek mathematician, once referred to the power of a lever by saying, "Give me somewhere to stand, and I will move the earth." Your children have provided you with this place to stand; now it's up to you to move the earth.

Archimedes' lever

Yes, we all want our children to learn new skills besides, for example, playing with a vacuum cleaner all day long. But the right thing to do is to fold our messages into their favorite activities. "Modulation" is what we need to do. So next let's explore modulation techniques.

Ivan loved dinosaurs. He loved watching dinosaur video clips, too. Back then, he couldn't stand to look at static pictures, and of course he couldn't identify the cartoon drawings representing Papa, Mami, Mindy, and Ivan that I have made for him. At this point, he did not even call me Papa. I knew from the therapists that his attention span for static objects was only a few seconds, so I needed to take advantage of those precious few seconds to teach him other things. I chose to insert four cartoon drawings of myself, my wife, Mindy, and Ivan into a dinosaur video clip. Each drawing appeared only for a short time (between three to five seconds), accompanied by some nonsensical voice-over from me, like: "Papaosaurus: PAPA!" "Mamiosaurus: MAMI!" "Mindyosaurus: MINDY!" and "Ivanosaurus: IVAN!"

Some frames from the dinosaur family video clip

This modulation of the dinosaur video with nonsensical frames was akin to commercials inserted by TV stations into their main programs: short enough to keep the audience focused, but long enough and frequent enough to convey the desired message. Sure, this video took me about two hours to make, but Ivan learned to recognize my drawings and learned to call me Papa. Of the numerous approaches tried by us, and by our therapists, this was still by far the fastest way to teach Ivan to call me Papa. The good thing about video clips is that you can play them over and over again. Once a video is made, the learning part usually happens quickly.

Let me recap the technique used here. Ivan loved to watch dinosaur video clips. But I did not just let him do that over and over again. I modulated in additional information, so he could acquire other skills. From my video clip, he learned to focus on static pictures/drawings, and also learned to call me Papa. That was no small feat! The dinosaur video frames were the anchor point, something that Ivan could hold on to. Without this anchor point, he would not have been able to learn the other skills.

Similarly, taking advantage of Ivan's obsession with the vacuum cleaner, I taught him many things, including verbalizing "I want vacuum!" loud and clear. Every time before I opened the closet and gave the vacuum cleaner to Ivan, I would make him go through one or two additional activities. I played the "fast" and "slow" running game with him. I taught him to go *tap, tap, tap* on his mother and say, "I am a good boy!" I taught him to read two-word expressions like "big sister," "big lion," "yellow banana," etc. He learned so many different things, all through his obsession with the vacuum cleaner. Those additional activities grew into standalone activities, and he no longer threw tantrums when he didn't get the vacuum cleaner. Best of all, Ivan and I became closer friends. Children understand when you put effort into speaking their language.

In the case of the vacuum cleaner, before I embarked on teaching Ivan additional skills, I did two things. First, I prepared a card album showing five steps involved in the play cycle of playing with the vacuum cleaner. Second, I scanned the cards of these five steps and modulated the drawings into one of Ivan's favorite video clips. I showed the modulated video clip to Ivan many times, and I also had the card album ready so I could remind him of the five steps of the play cycle. The first couple of times when I put the vacuum cleaner back into the closet, Ivan grew very anxious. But I kept showing him the card album to let him know that he could get the vacuum cleaner any time, but that we needed to put the vacuum cleaner back in its place at the end of the cycle. I especially wanted him to familiarize himself with the part where we put the vacuum cleaner back into the closet.

Ivan's card album for the vacuum cleaner play cycle

Very soon he got used to the five steps of the play cycle, and as a matter of fact he thought it was fun to see me put the vacuum cleaner back into the closet. After he had achieved that milestone I started to insert another activity: I ran one loop around the staircase, and asked him to follow me. After he completed the loop, I allowed him to ask me for the vacuum cleaner. After a couple of times, I switched to a different activity and made him go *tap, tap, tap* on his mother and say, "I am a good boy." Then I moved to teaching him to read two-word expressions, and so on. It was all fun for him, but he learned many different things, day after day, and became less and less attached to the vacuum cleaner.

I told my wife that it was a win-win situation for us. If he was still obsessed with the vacuum cleaner, I could keep teaching him more skills. And if he was no longer obsessed with the vacuum cleaner, then we would win the battle regarding his obsession. As it turned out, we won both ways: Ivan learned many other skills, and his obsession for the vacuum cleaner also subsided.

Why do pro-video children stop or reduce a repetitive behavior when the behavior is connected to other processes? I believe this is because we have provided a way for their thoughts to flow to other topics, a way for them to pay attention to other things. In a sense, we have helped them to develop a capability to "feel bored" from repetitive activities.

So, let me recap. Process modulation is the natural way of teaching additional skills to pro-video children. In the case of video editing, you can insert short clips anywhere in the video. In the case of real-life repetitive behaviors, you can modulate in additional processes at the beginning of the repetitive behavior. Let me put it more clearly: (a) for processes that are under your control, like video clips, you can modulate in other processes (including static concepts) at any point, and (b) for processes that are under the child's control, like a behavior in which the child engages, you should modulate in other processes at the beginning, prior to the child engaging the behavior. The main process serves as the anchor point from which the child can learn new skills. The additional processes should be as brief as TV commercials and not overtake the main program. If the commercials are longer than the main TV program, nobody will want to watch them. The same idea applies to process modulation.

Archimedes was right. You can move the earth. Your children have provided you with that place to stand. Our children are waiting to connect with us—they are telling us "Here is the door to my world, please come on in." We need to learn to listen to our children, in their language.

Stimming Time is Learning Time

There are many kinds of repetitive behaviors. The longer cycle-duration ones are called repetitive plays, like Ivan's playing with the vacuum cleaner for hours. The shorter cycle-duration ones are known as "stims" or "stimming," which stands for "self-stimulation." This distinction is not strict. You will find me using the word "stim" to refer to both types of repetitive behaviors. Stims come in a variety of forms: spinning, rocking, hand flapping, spitting, mouthing, repetition of words, object-gripping (like holding a spoon at all times), etc. Functionally, stims have many causes and serve different purposes. They may help people with autism manage their emotions or deal with sensory issues. My two children and Tisa's brother's children have each had some stimming behaviors. Mindy used to do some hand flapping. Tin loved to line up dominos, and Ivan did the same to a lesser degree. Ivan and Pi have spun, tiptoed, and hand flapped, among other things. Ivan used to hold a spoon wherever he went: both at home and when going out. He even needed the spoon to go to bed. Holding the spoon had a soothing effect on him. Ivan moved on from spoon gripping to mouthing for a time, and would constantly bite his shirt or sleeve.

There are two detrimental things that adults can do in response to their children's repetitive behaviors. The absolute worst thing to do is to try to suppress these behaviors—we shouldn't interfere with the fundamental signal units of pro-video manifestations. The second worst thing to do is to ignore these behaviors. The children are pleading with you to come into their world, and you are ignoring their pleas!

So please enter their world. Participate with them. Use their behaviors as a place to stand, so you can move the earth for them. Stimming time is learning time. Stims are the fundamental signal units of pro-video thinking and capture the moment of maximum attention of these children. If we don't teach them at their moment of maximum attention, then when will we teach them? Talk to them through their eyes. They will appreciate you speaking their language.

We live in an information age. We enjoy high-tech devices such as cell phones, radios, televisions, and internet-connected computers. All modern electronic signals actually come to us through a modulation process. Signal modulation paves today's information superhighway, and I believe it can pave the superhighway to communicating with our children with autism as well. The following diagram explains mathematically the modulation procedure in the process space. To the left, we see the vital intellectual concepts for children to learn. But we have problems communicating our message because those concepts are (a) too narrowly defined in the concept space, hence too broadly distributed in the process space; and (b) in a region that doesn't resonate with our children. Therefore, our children with autism cannot digest our message. To the right, we have a stimming behavior, which is a Dirac delta in the process space. Modulation means that we use the stimming behavior as our "carrier signal," and we intertwine it with our original message in an operation known as "convolution." With this operation, we achieve two objectives: (a) the vital concepts now resonate with our children and are readily digested, and (b) the modulated process diverts energy from the stimming behavior, connecting it to other areas of the brain. The Dirac delta is no more.

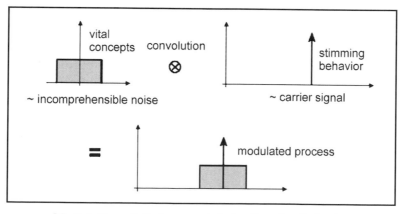

Modulation of vital concepts into stimming behavior

72

As a side note, convolution is the mathematical operation in the momentum space, while modulation is the corresponding operation in the coordinate space. That is, they are two sides of the same coin.

Without modulation, our message is noise to our children, and their stimming behavior is noise to us. With modulation, our children learn, and their stimming behavior stops. Is this magic? You bet!

Sensory Problems

In the middle of the night, when all is quiet, you can turn on your home stereo to play some music and realize that, even when it is playing at a very low volume, you can hear it. If you turn the volume on the stereo up, you might wake up your family members or even your neighbors, and they will get very mad at you. However, playing your music at the same loud volume during the daytime may not be an issue.

People with autism often have sensory problems: the volume of sensory input inside their brains is just too loud. But we know that loudness is relative. We don't mind some background noise during the day, right?

In light of what we have talked about regarding pro-video children as being focused on processes, and about regarding repetitive behaviors as building blocks, I believe that the same applies to the sensory system of people with autism. It's not that the sensory signals are too loud—it's simply that the sensory part of the brain is not connected to other processes. Just as some parents view stimming as something negative, when it can, in fact, be an opportunity to teach their children other vital skills, I would say most people view the sensory issues in children with autism as medical problems. Therefore, we often believe that external signals need to be suppressed or avoided, and we sometimes give the children medications or protective gears.

People typically do not try to view these sensory problems as something positive, as the door into the autistic child's world. So they don't see these sensory problems as opportunities to link additional processes into children's routines, to establish more connections inside their brains. Sensory processes are a particular subset of all processes inside a child's brain. Sensory problems and repetitive behaviors have a common origin: they are isolated entities inside the momentum space of a child's brain. Children suffer sensory problems because they devote their full attention to one single area of their brains.

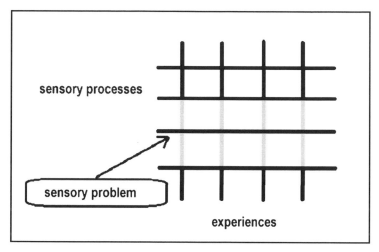

Sensory problems: sensory processes not connected to other experiences

Sensory problems are there because of a lack of context of the outside signals. This points to the solution of sensory problems: we need to connect the problematic signals to other experiences of the children—hopefully positive experiences. I believe that once enough connections are established, the sensory problems will go away.

Let me provide a few examples of sensory problems and how they went away. When I was young, I really did not like songs with lyrics. I much preferred instrumental music. To me, songs were too complicated, and the human voice kind of ruined the purity of the music. For the same reason, I liked cartoons and comic strips—they are simpler than human-actor movies. I found it odd that most radio stations played songs but not instrumental music. Why did so few people out there share my liking? With age—late into my college years—I became more receptive to songs. After I started to learn some foreign languages, I finally started to enjoy all types of songs. Compared to typical people, it took me forever to get to where everyone else was. In this example, my interest in foreign languages (English, French and German) facilitated my liking of songs with lyrics.

In another example of sensory overload, when Mindy was three years old, I took her to Chuck E. Cheese's, a children's games-and-rides place that also served food. She was so startled that I had to get her out of the place after five minutes, wasting all the game tokens. By age five, however, Mindy could handle all kinds of noises, and she really enjoyed the games at Chuck E. Cheese's. I also remember Mindy's first Halloween. I took her around the neighborhood for trick-or-treating, she got spooked at the very first house, and that was it. This last Halloween, she was comfortable visiting many houses. She still got spooked at the last house when a skull suddenly talked to her, but she kind of enjoyed it and could laugh it off. In the case of Chuck E. Cheese's, Mindy had a friend's birthday party thrown there, so it was fun for her. In the case of Halloween, she participated in a daytime trick-or-treating in school, so she was exposed to trick-or-treating and Halloween costumes in a gentler environment beforehand.

Where am I going with all these stories? I believe that as more connections are established inside our brains, when positive contexts are linked to the problem signals, we can learn to handle these signals better, and even learn to enjoy them.

Ivan also had sensory problems with noises; he would cry when he heard loud noises or when someone talked too loud. But with time he did get better. Ivan also had issues with physical touching: whereas Mindy enjoyed being hugged, Ivan hated it. Again, with time, Ivan did get used to hugging. In my experience, children with autism can indeed overcome their sensory problems, and become accustomed to noise and physical contact (e.g., clapping hands or holding hands). The key is to make their experience fun. When Ivan started in a new school, he didn't participate in his music class in school: he disliked clapping his hands, or holding classmates' hands and dancing in a circle. With patience, video clips (the music teacher was very kind to supply us with her video clips, and I also searched for children's line dancing video clips on YouTube and other sites), and a lot of practice at home with me dancing and clapping, Ivan got used to the music class activities and was finally able to participate in class and enjoy it, at least from time to time. The first time Ivan held his friends' hands and danced in a circle, I couldn't believe my eyes. I captured it on my smartphone and shared my excitement with my wife. Trust me: with hard work and patience, things do get better.

I think it may be worthwhile to view at least some of the sensory problems from a positive angle. Instead of assuming that there is something wrong with the children, let's take a step back. We can connect positive activities to our children's sensory experiences. This way, connections can be established to other areas inside their brains. Once the connections are established, the energy from the brain signals is free to flow to somewhere else, and the hyper-sensitivity issues will go away. To me, avoiding sensory stimuli is not the answer. Modulation is the key.

Both stimming behaviors and sensory problems therefore have a common origin: signal amplification due to auto-feedback of an overly connected brain. However, there is a difference. Stimming behaviors are connected to the "attractive" center of the brain, so the children with autism will continue to repeat these behaviors. Sensory problems on the other hand are connected to the "repulsive" center of the brain, so the children will try to avoid those external sensory signals. I believe that in both cases modulation is the key, but the directions of modulation should be opposite. In the case of stimming behaviors, we modulate in additional activities to those repetitive behaviors. In the case of sensory problems, we should instead start from other fun activities, and modulate in the problematic signals gently and gradually.

To summarize, no matter whether it's repetitive behaviors or sensory problems, children with autism are simply trying to tell us: "Here is the door to my world. Please come on in." These are the areas where their reception of signals is at its finest, and potentially can be leveraged towards the development of their talents. For example: I said I did not like songs with lyrics, right? Interestingly, you will find a lullaby at the end of this book. Granted, I am not the greatest songwriter ever, but I did write and sing personalized songs for my wife and for my children. Even Mozart, Neruda, and Pavarotti combined can't beat me on that...I've come a long way, haven't I?

Skip the Question and Do the Action

There is an old fable about "The Ant and the Grasshopper." The ant spent the warm season working hard, while the grasshopper sang and played every day. When the winter came, the grasshopper suffered.

Parents of children with autism often ask questions like:

- Why does my child spin around?
- Why does my child roll his head?
- Why does my child walk on tiptoes?
- Why does my child flap her hands?
- Why does my child follow a certain ritual?
- Why does my child line up toys?
- Why does my child spit?
- Why does my child make this weird noise?
- Why does my child play with the vacuum cleaner all day long?
- Why does my child scream repeatedly?
- Why does my child go crazy in response to noise?
- Why does my child go crazy with fluorescent light?
- Why does my child hold a spoon all day and all night?
- Why does my child sing songs in the middle of the night?
- Why does my child eat his shirt?
- Why does my child lick?
- Why does my child stick his whole hand into his mouth?
- Why does my child bang her head?
- Why does my child keep playing the same game over and over again?
- Why does my child keep watching the same video clip over and over again?

And so on.

What I see is that while the children are busy performing repetitive behaviors, the parents are busy trying to find an explanation. This parent response is extremely detrimental to the development of their pro-video children.

Trying to find explanations for the large varieties of repetitive behaviors is akin to asking the question, "Why is a chair called a chair? Why isn't it called a potato?" In the momentum space, repetitive behaviors are fundamental entities, just like the concept of a "chair" is a fundamental entity in the coordinate space of verbal communication. In the same way that it is a waste of time to philosophize about why a chair is called a chair, it is a waste of time to dig into explanations for the repetitive behaviors of pro-video children.

When parents philosophize, recession happens. It's just that in this case, we are talking about recession in the development of their children. I gave up asking the "why" questions right after I understood Ivan: right after I saw the true nature of the repetitive behaviors in the momentum space. It is pointless to ask the why. Instead, now every time I see a repetitive behavior in any children with autism, I get excited. It's their way of telling us: "Here is the door to my world, please come on in." I don't see repetitive behaviors per se any more: I see Archimedes' lever. I see opportunity.

When we spent time with other autistic families, I saw some parents becoming uneasy and embarrassed about their children's stimming behaviors. I guess it was hard for other people to understand why I got all excited in front of them. I felt so sorry for these children: they have been pleading with their parents to come into their world, but the parents just did not know how to listen to their children.

Instead of asking "why," parents should be asking "what" and "how," as in: "What skills should my child learn?" and "How can I teach these skills to my child?"

My advice to parents is to skip the "why" questions and act. Modulate additional processes into the children's repetitive behaviors, so that they can learn some vital skills. Every minute counts. At the end of the next chapter you will find a list of some vital skills. Don't let the golden opportunities of repetitive behaviors slip away. Your children have an endless list of skills that they need to learn. It is simply unacceptable to say: "I don't know what to teach my child." If you need a focus point, or if you sometimes are at a loss as to what skills to teach your children, then just teach them to read. Yes, teach them to read single words like "banana" or "apple," and move to verbs like "push" or "pull," then move to simple sentences like: "How are you?" "I am good." "What's your name?" "How old are you?" Then move to longer sentences. Write down the words on blank index cards or on a piece of paper, and draw a picture if at all possible. If your children still cannot focus on index cards, then fall back to video clips: modulate static frames into their favorite video clips, so you can teach them some initial pro-picture skills. Store these video clips on your computer, TV set, tablet PC, or smartphone if necessary, so you can have them handy at any moment.

Escapism Part 1: The Experience in LIVE

Although I have not described the acronym LIVE thus far, I consider the importance of the "Experience" component for pro-video children so paramount that I have decided to include it in this section.

LIVE stands for Letters, Images, Voice, and Experience. *Letters* means that children with autism should learn to read early on, because they are visually oriented. *Images* means our messages are best conveyed to children with autism through pictures and video clips. *Voice* means parents' familiar voices should be used in picture-aided talking and in video clips. *Experience* means we teach our children with autism based on their individual experiences: we focus on their individual interests—on their personal life story.

It is easy to neglect the letter E in LIVE. We often have preconceived notions about what our children should be learning. We look at development milestone guidelines and impose them on our children. For typical children, we often succeed with our goals. However, with children with autism, both parents and children often feel tremendously frustrated because the set learning goals cannot be achieved no matter how much effort the parents put in. This results in friction between parents and children, and the parent-child relationship suffers. The worst outcome is that the children get discouraged, and try to escape from future learning settings. The children become less and less compliant; the parents become more and more frustrated. And the vicious cycle goes on and on, making everyone miserable.

I think the description above resonates with many families with children with autism. This is especially true in families with pro-video children. If you observe that your children are drifting from one activity to another; if you realize that your children are avoiding and escaping from your teaching moments; if you have followed the first three letters in *LIVE* but are getting minimal return on your teaching investment; then step back a moment and see whether you are missing the last element of *LIVE*: the letter *E*, for experience.

I mentioned earlier that stimming time means learning time. But what if the child has developed escapism?

How can we teach our children if they are escaping? If there is no escapism, we can teach them any skill. But if they have developed full-blown escapism, if they are drifting from one activity to another, or are losing interest and losing focus, then we should listen to our children's signals, and stop pushing white noise that they cannot absorb.

All children have their own interests. If escapism is present, we should take a step back and anchor our messages to their interests. It is for exactly this reason that I don't think third-party games or books can achieve much in teaching children with autism in their early stages of life. Your teaching material must be attached to their immediate life experience.

When Ivan was young, he developed some symptoms of escapism at one point, and was not focusing and reading as well as he did before.

I grew concerned. I realized that he was confronted with too many words and was getting confused. He became hesitant when sounding out words, and was afraid of making mistakes. When I wrote out words for him on index cards or on the magnetic drawing board, I realized he wasn't focusing as well as he did before. Information overloading, I guessed. Sometimes with learning processes, things tend to get murkier before they get clear again.

It took one particular learning event to remind me what was missing. Mindy and Ivan were repeatedly watching a video clip of the song "Stand by Me" from the animated movie *The Lion King*. The two of them memorized the entire song and sang it together. Ivan was mispronouncing the name of one of the characters, Pumbaa, as "Kumaa." I picked up the magnetic drawing board and spelled "PUMBAA" for Ivan to correct him. Knowing Ivan had been presenting signs of escapism, I was not expecting him to make the correction. However, he did make the correction! Then it hit me: I had been forgetting about the letter *E* in *LIVE*. When you teach children something closely related to their interests—something attached to the children's experience or to the children's focus of attention—they can learn, and very well. When I wrote down sentences from the song's lyrics on the magnetic drawing board, Ivan could read them, too. So I found a new anchor to teach him new things. For instance, some of the song lyrics were "...and the land is dark," so I wrote down the words DARK and BRIGHT on index cards with some drawings (a dark night with the moon, and a bright lamp). And then we played a game, where I asked Ivan to turn the power switch on and off to make a room dark or bright. Ivan loved the game and repeated the words DARK and BRIGHT whenever he flipped the switches. So he learned to say and to read these two words, and also to follow my verbal command to turn the lights on or off.

Children's experiences matter. When your children are developing signs of escapism, take a step back and stick to your children's favorite experiences. Use them as anchor points and teach them things immediately related to those experiences. Rest assured that your children will always provide you with plenty of such anchor points, plenty of places for you to apply your Archimedes' lever. Also, immediate intervention is crucial to preventing escapism. You need to help your children grow their knowledge and skills from their anchor points, because that's the way children with autism learn, modulating new signals onto an existing carrier backbone. If intervention happens too late, these children won't have developed a foundation for learning additional skills, and discouragement and escapism will ensue. Don't give up when you observe escapism. Take a deep breath, step back, and find that last letter E in $LIVE$. Make up for the time lost, and use your children's life experiences as your anchor point. Remember, each child learns things differently. Children with autism may have unconventional ways of learning, but they also have unconventional talents. If a battle is too hard to fight today, take a break and fight it another day. Use today to teach your children something that they can relate to, something that they are interested in and can absorb, and expand from there.

Escapism Part 2: Personal Attention and Touch

When Ivan was three and half, I became extremely busy at work. At that time, Ivan also happened to switch from individualized ABA services to a group ABA classroom setting. This was because Ivan was making progress at a good pace, and we thought it was the appropriate time for him to start socializing with other children. However, after joining the group ABA classroom, Ivan's progress stalled. I was so busy at work that for a few months I just did not have enough time to interact closely with Ivan or with his teachers and therapists in school. Ivan developed significant escapism and actually regressed in some of his skills, at which point I became alarmed.

Once more, I needed to scratch my head and try to figure out what went wrong.

Right around that time we took a big family vacation. Ivan had a blast on vacation, because he enjoyed the attention of so many adults and cousins. As we later found out, right after the vacation, his response at school climbed back up a little bit. He still presented escapism, though. It was frustrating. He was even escaping from some of the new video clips I made for him. I was willing to accept his escapism from activities like reading books or looking at pictures. But escapism from watching video clips? Something was clearly and terribly wrong.

That was the moment that I told myself: enough is enough. I needed to spend some time with Ivan. So on one particular Saturday, I did nothing but to hang out with Ivan. I took him to the local shopping mall in our neighborhood. I took him to McDonald's. I took him to go ride the elevators and escalators, and to play in the water fountain. I took him shopping at the grocery store, where they had these very cute child-sized shopping carts that Ivan could push around. I took him to a local bookstore. I spent the whole day with him, and took plenty of pictures of each moment of these activities. Ivan had fun that day.

That night I made a video clip of our experience, including speech bubbles in first person. The next morning I showed the video clip to Ivan. At first he attempted to escape from watching the video, but he quickly recognized the sequence of events: McDonald's, elevator, escalator, water fountain, shopping cart, home, etc. And all of that caught his attention. Then he stayed through the entire video clip. I could tell that I was gaining him back.

Later that Sunday evening, he really enjoyed watching the new video clip, and kept saying "I want more," meaning that he wanted to watch the same video clip again. After replaying the new video all too many times, I switched to show him one of the other new video clips that I had made earlier, and which he had not wanted to watch. (In that video, I animated a toy school bus going on a track that Ivan needed to assemble, and the video was supposed to teach Ivan to say "no good" and "yeah.") And then, a miracle happened: he no longer escaped. As a matter of fact, he enjoyed it, and he memorized the voice-overs of the whole video. Moreover, that video clip had some spelling in it, too, and Ivan was able to focus on the words again. That meant Ivan had started to recover some of his reading skills.

So I gained my son back, one more time.

Throughout the process, I was not working blindly or trying out techniques randomly. No, I was working with a very clear guiding principle in my mind. I have observed in pro-video children and adults that this subgroup of people with autism seem to perform best when they have the full personalized attention of other people. That is, they enjoy and need undivided attention from their parents and therapists. So escapism may actually not be caused by a learning disability, but rather be a consequence of a lack of personalized attention. Remember that these children have long memories, as if they carry an accountant's **double-entry ledger** inside their brains to keep track of their good experiences and bad experiences. We need to suppress their resentment before it becomes permanent. Escapism could be a way that pro-video children protest a lack of necessary attention. They are saying: "I need your love and attention." And we, the adults, should listen.

Ivan enjoyed close interaction with his therapists when he had one-on-one ABA services. I guess the jump into group-based ABA was too much of a change for him. This, coupled with my very busy work schedule during those few months, meant a disaster in his learning progress. This experience with Ivan suggests to me that pro-video children should have close and personal attention throughout early childhood, until they can verbalize.

Another vital part of working with pro-video children is the "tactile" component. My brother-in-law Pham, a pro-video person, gives the following advice about teaching pro-video children: you need to make things fun. No static objects. Things need to be moving, colorful, fun, and you need to rely on all five senses. In particular, he pointed out that the sense of touch is very important. You should incorporate objects or activities with a "touch" aspect. This certainly was very true with Ivan. I recaptured his attention by playing the "elevator game" with him: we would either use our closet's sliding doors or two pieces of luggage to simulate an elevator's doors, and then Ivan would pretend to press a button, and I would lift him up and down to emulate the motion of an elevator. He loved the game a lot. Dancing, jumping, hand clapping, finger touching, nose touching, and forehead touching are all good games to play. Pro-video children need to have some sort of "touch-fun" connection, in addition to a purely visual component.

Fear Conquering: The Elevator Story

The elevator story is actually more elaborate. When Ivan was first exposed to elevators and escalators, he liked escalators quite a bit. As for elevators, he was indifferent. That changed the first time I took him to a ride in a glass elevator. A glass elevator is a see-through elevator. You could see what an elevator really did: that it went up and down, and that you were lifted above the ground when you rode it. That freaked Ivan out. For the next few months, Ivan simply refused to take any elevator, whether they were see-through or enclosed. Despite his refusal to ride them, he was very curious about how elevators worked, and would spend a long time in malls sitting and watching elevators in action. He particularly liked the see-through ones where you could see the mechanical gears in action. I noticed his curiosity and started to play the elevator game with him, pretending that our walk-in closet was the elevator. He enjoyed the game very much.

My wife found some toys which contained elevators. One was a fire station, and another one was a parking garage. Ivan's elevator fascination did not stop there. My wife discovered tons of elevator videos on YouTube. It was crazy. Ivan's passion was obviously shared by many people: there was an endless supply of elevator videos on YouTube. We couldn't believe it—so many people out there had nothing better to do than taking video clips of elevators! Ivan must have watched hundreds of those video clips. I particularly recommend the videos from "DieselDucy"—Mr. Andrew Reams in real life, an adult with Asperger's, and the most famous "elevator photographer" on YouTube. I am so grateful to him. Ivan learned to say many sentences from those videos. Playing with elevator toys and watching elevator video clips became Ivan's new stimming behavior.

For a few months Ivan did not ride in elevators, in part because we lived in suburbia, and elevators were simply not very common. Most shopping malls had escalators anyway. One day I took Ivan to my office and the only way up was the elevator (taking the stairs would have required too much effort for Ivan). I was hesitating until I saw

Ivan run to the elevator and press the button. And he enjoyed the ride. Well, that was a good sign, I told myself. It was an enclosed elevator, though, so I wasn't sure whether he would still be afraid of the see-through ones. My doubts disappeared a few weekends later. When we went to a mall, Ivan actually also ran to the see-through elevator and pressed the button himself. He was no longer scared of elevator rides. He now enjoyed watching himself being lifted above the ground. In the process of getting used to elevator rides, Ivan trained himself exclusively through visual means. He became familiar with elevators and lost his fear simply by watching YouTube video clips. I must admit that it did not cross my mind that Ivan would lose his fear to elevators that way. Ivan did all the training himself!

Stopping the Crying: Part 1

Due to the nature of my work, I interact with colleagues around the globe. Needless to say, my sleep schedule is sometimes chaotic. On one particular day, by dinner time I was exhausted. I excused myself to my wife, skipped dinner, and collapsed in bed.

I must have been asleep for two hours or so when I woke up to the sound of Ivan crying loudly. It was a disaster in the house: Ivan was throwing a tantrum and crying non-stop, and my wife was totally helpless and visibly frustrated.

Realizing the severity of the situation, I placed my hands on Ivan's shoulders and looked at him straight in the eye. My wife watched me mumble something. In about twenty seconds Ivan stopped crying completely. And there was peace in the house again. Yes, in twenty seconds the tantrum was gone. Only after Ivan calmed down could my wife sit down and soothe him, and have some quality mother-son time that evening.

That was one of my proudest moments as a parent of children with autism. That night, my wife asked me how I managed to calm Ivan down. I told her, I simply asked Ivan one question three times, calmly and gently. And the question was: "What did Papa say?" After repeating this question three times, Ivan stopped crying. It worked like magic.

Here is the background story to this magical moment.

Very often, when Ivan or Mindy cried, I would tell them "big boys don't cry" or "big girls don't cry." Then I would soothe them, sometimes draw pictures for them, and go through the circumstances that caused their crying. However, despite doing a lot of picture talking with Ivan and telling him "big boys don't cry," I felt that he still did not understand my message.

Well, communication takes time. I know the precise day when he finally understood my message. That day, we took Mindy and Ivan to a birthday party of a friend of theirs. After the party, on the way home, we stopped by a gas station to put some gas in the car. It so happened that this gas station had a car wash facility, a fact that did not escape Ivan's attention. Ivan hated car washes: they were too scary for him. Ivan then thought that we were going to go through the car wash, and started to cry and threw a tantrum. I kept saying "big boys don't cry" to him and reassured him that today we were not doing the car wash. I told him "no, no car wash," but he still didn't understand, and kept saying "I don't like car wash!"

I did a few things. I recorded Ivan's crying on my smartphone's video camera. After we came home, I did some picture talking with Ivan. I drew a picture of the birthday party and reminded him that the party was fun and that he liked the "bouncie houses" (inflatable castles where children could jump inside). And then I drew a picture of the gas station, drew the car wash facility, showed him the video where he was crying, and reminded him that "no, no car wash" (meaning that we were not doing the car wash that day), and wrote down "big boys don't cry." Then I gave him a hug and did a high five with him. I was simply communicating to him that there was no need to cry because we were not doing the car wash that day.

I knew at that moment that he understood my message: that there was truly no reason for him to cry when I told him so. And that was why he stopped crying the next time when I asked him "What did Papa say?"

So, what lesson can we draw from this experience? First of all, I believe that communication takes time. We cannot wait until tantrums happen to seek a solution. Ivan stopped crying not because I asked him "What did Papa say?" but because of our earlier communication. Secondly, very often tantrums happen because of a misunderstanding. For pro-video children, a combination of video and picture talking in the evening will help them to clarify their misunderstanding. Remember that children with autism are visual—verbal communication is simply not enough. You need to communicate with them through their eyes. Take each instance of tantrum as an opportunity to do picture talking with your children in the evening.

Stopping the Crying: Part 2

Children with autism have powerful brains, and signals inside their brains are amplified. Very often, these children cry simply because the emotional signals are too strong. Because their mind is going over the same incident repeatedly, their crying could last forever. In this case, it often does not help to ask them about the reason why they cry, nor does it help to ask them what they want. The more you ask about the incident, the worse it gets. This is because you are not helping them get away from the subject.

In this type of crying, your children are simply trying to tell you: **"Please help me get out of this loop, these signals inside my brain are too intense!"**

That's all.

For Mindy, very often it helps if I sit down with her and draw pictures. I may simply draw a picture of a flower, or a house, or a tree, or the sky with clouds, etc. Something totally unrelated to the incident that has caused her to cry. All she needs is something to distract her mind, so she can refocus.

And there is also the ultimate "nuclear" option. Thank goodness for modern technology. A smartphone comes in handy. It works for both Mindy and Ivan. I would let Mindy play some games, or let Ivan watch some elevator or car wash videos, and their crying would subside immediately.

You may be worried that children may soon learn to exploit this venue and fake crying in order to play with the phone. Well, as I have explained elsewhere in the book, children with autism have much less sense of self and are much less likely to be as "street smart" as their neurotypical peers. If your children are faking crying to get your smartphone, then, congratulations, your children are developing neurotypical skills. In that case you can limit the duration and/or the number of video clips they are allowed to watch. I would say that before you get to that point, please do not hesitate to use a smartphone or computer to disconnect your children from their suffering.

Lining Up and Waiting for a Turn

To line up and wait for their turn is an exceptionally difficult task for many pro-video children. When Ivan was four years old, he attended a regular (meaning non-special education) preschool twice a week. They had gymnastics class every Wednesday. Very quickly Ivan's teachers expressed concerns and called for a parent-teacher meeting. They told my wife and me the problems they encountered with Ivan. Among these problems, one was that Ivan couldn't participate in the gymnastics class, because he was always running around and couldn't line up and wait for his turn. They also told my wife that Ivan would benefit from an aide for other classroom activities.

I had to calm the teachers down. I told them the purpose of Ivan attending a regular children's preschool was for him to observe and get used to what the typical children do. I told them that frankly I had no expectations on the socialization part. (I did not tell them that that was not a priority to me anyway.) I told them that as far as classroom activities went, my only request was that they focused on teaching Ivan to doodle and paint. As for an aide, my wife volunteered to act as one for Ivan.

So my wife started to go to school with Ivan. She told me what happened in the gymnastics class. It was a complete circus. The two teachers plus my wife—three adults—had to chase after Ivan to get him to line up, with virtually no success. They needed help. I took a couple of hours off from work and went to Ivan's school. If I wasn't there, holding Ivan and forcing him to wait for his turn to do the exercises (bar and rings, vaulting, pencil roll, back flip, balance beam, etc.), Ivan would either be running around or rolling on the grass. All in all, I would rate Ivan's compliance at a 5% level. I took some pictures of Ivan participating in the gymnastics class, and promised the teachers that I would make a video clip to deal with the problem.

Now, mind you, asking Ivan, a hyperactive, pro-video child, to hold nice and still in a fixed spot was akin to asking a cat to swim: it's against their nature. How in the world could I make a video to teach Ivan to hold still and wait for his turn?

Sometimes when a problem is tough, you shouldn't face it head on. My train of thought went in two directions:

1.   I thought I could hedge my bets: I could make a video to teach Ivan some other vital skills from this experience, just in case he did not learn to line up and wait for his turn.
2.   I remembered what Ivan's uncle Pham told me: pro-video people like himself learn best when things are fun, when things involve all five senses.

So I told myself, I am not going to make a video to tell Ivan that he *should* line up. Instead, I am going to teach him that lining up is *fun*. Now you might say, "Who was are you kidding? Lining up is fun?" I considered the other point to draw some inspiration. I told myself, let's find a fun skill to teach Ivan.

I decided to teach Ivan about associative imagination. I settled for introducing Ivan to the expression "is like." So I made a video, and the title was "IS LIKE." The first part of the video clip was to set up fun associations unrelated to lining up. I had couple of frames to show Ivan that:

• Playing on the rings was like swinging like a gorilla.
• Vaulting was like jumping like a kangaroo.

90

- Walking on the balance beam was like walking like a crab.
- Performing the pencil roll was like rolling a pencil.

I decided that preamble should catch Ivan's attention and make it fun for him. I followed up with the main subject:

- Lining up was like five little cars: I made an animation of five children (including Ivan) popping into the scene lining up, followed by five toy cars of different colors popping into the scene.
- Lining up was like five little speckled frogs: again, five children popping into the scene and lining up, followed by five little speckled frogs popping into the scene. (See next figure. Notice that I intentionally used "LINE UP" instead of "LINING UP," because I also wanted to use this term as a verbal command for Ivan. For children with autism, functionality trumps grammatical correctness.)

As for the negative part about rolling on the grass, I saved it for last:

- A static picture of Ivan rolling on the grass, with an image of Papa popping up into the scene telling Ivan that "rolling on grass is like...NOT NICE!" and "Papa says No, No, No!"

This video took longer than usual to produce because it had more animation. It took me about three days to finalize, about four hours altogether.

It was a visual success for Ivan at home. Ivan liked the new video. But we weren't sure how effective it was going to be for the real gymnastics class. The following Wednesday, when Ivan had gymnastics class again, I showed him the video on TV that morning, and later again on my smartphone, right before the class.

The result was about 70% successful, in my opinion. Ivan went from being totally incapable of staying in line, to staying in line most of the time. The teachers immediately noticed the change: Ivan was staying in line by himself, at last, and for a very long time!

Some frames from the "IS LIKE" video clip

Sure, Ivan became less compliant towards the end of the 30-minute class. I had to intervene a few times to remind him that "line up" was like five little cars or five little speckled frogs, and that rolling on the grass was not nice and Papa said no, no, no. Each time I could see Ivan really making an effort to follow my request. Overall, I would rate it a success. Not bad at all for the first session after video communication. The cat was swimming in the water now.

So I turned to my wife and asked her: "Did you see Ivan? He was lining up and waiting for his turn!" And she told me that the teachers also noticed the change. Then I asked my wife: "So do you think autism is a behavioral problem or a communication problem?" She nodded and agreed: "A communication problem."

By the next gymnastics class, Ivan was 90% compliant according to my assessment. That is, indistinguishable from some of the naughty typical boys. Best of all, he didn't roll on the grass anymore. That's zero, nil, nada. Voilà: success. From then on, I did not need to go to Ivan's gymnastics class. The gymnastics teachers could get Ivan back in line on their own, without assistance from other teachers or from my wife.

I did not go to the next session, but from my wife's description, Ivan was probably 95% compliant. That is, there was virtually no need for intervention, except for a few verbal reminders from the gymnastics teachers. Ivan's behavior was the same as the normal behavior of many boys in the class.

From a seemingly impossible situation, there was now a solution. Ivan could finally participate and enjoy the gymnastics class by himself, and no more headaches for the teachers.

Children with autism are perfectly fine the way they are. Time and again I have proven that once instructions are properly communicated, these children can learn and accommodate your requests. Those issues that many people call "behavioral problems" all but disappear after these children understand your message. I mean, what most people do to "handle" children with autism is to give them verbal commands, and then the adults get frustrated because these children do not follow those verbal commands. We adults need to change our approach, understand the native language of these children, and make an effort to communicate with them in their language.

When you properly communicate your message, children with autism can fully understand it, and they may even surprise you with their maturity. For instance, Ivan memorized every single passage, every single frame of the gymnastics video clip I made for him. He would often recite the sentences from this video clip, except that he always skipped the sentences about "five little cars" and "five little speckled frogs." That is, he perfectly understood that there was an underlying message behind those funny sentences. He could tell my intention. He could tell that the real intention behind those funny words was his Papa's plea to him to get in line like the other children. And he complied. He knew the right thing to do, without me needing to tell him explicitly.

93

Music Class

Another challenge for Ivan was his lack of participation in his music class. Music class uses many strategies that are absent in visual learning. In music class, children participate by singing, by clapping their hands, and by holding hands to dance in a circle. That is, a lot of information exchange is sensory in nature, involving auditory and tactile/physical stimuli. Though Ivan usually does enjoy music, the combination of loud volume with all the social activities was overwhelming for him. Ivan refused to participate in any of the music class activities, and preferred to just sit it out as an observer.

That reminded me of how I participated in parties as a teenager. I hated dancing. Though I was a social person and often attended my friends' parties, dancing was not my thing. I enjoyed the loud music, but there was no way I would go into the crowd and shake my body. I was an oddball at those parties. I thought that I was hopelessly different from the rest of the world, until I went into my PhD program. Then I realized I was normal within that crowd. Yes, my friends in the PhD program threw parties, too (and I myself have hosted some parties as well, believe it or not). But, unlike the parties in my high school and college days, most of my PhD classmates did not dance, either. We just enjoyed munching on food, chatting, and listening to music. Sometimes we watched movies, other times we held barbecues. Those were the kind of parties we enjoyed.

Though I could understand Ivan's refusal to participate in music class activities from my own experience, I thought that participation in auditory and sensory activities was still beneficial for him. Besides, that was the whole purpose of the music class: to provide sensory experiences not readily available in regular class activities. Ivan was not the only child that was shy about participating in music class: some typical children also felt uncomfortable participating. I knew the whole purpose of the music class was to eventually get everyone to participate. We are not talking about hard rock style music or moves, but mellow children's music, skipping, circle dancing, hand holding, and hand clapping.

Unfortunately, I became ill right around the time I wanted to help Ivan with his music class. Not so ill that I couldn't attend music class with him, but I simply did not have the energy or the creativity to make cartoon videos for him. I had to reduce my video clips to three sources: (a) music class videos supplied by the music teacher (I was so glad that the music teacher was such a nice person and ready to help out with Ivan's case), (b) video clips captured on my smartphone, and (c) whatever I could find on YouTube and other websites. Anyway, this was the first time that I worked with Ivan on sensory issues instead of video-memory issues, so I did not place high hopes on the task. I simply tried to hold his hands to dance in a circle with me, and teach him to clap his hands, too.

Around age of four, Ivan was really making progress in his music class. One week, I finally saw Ivan clapping his hands in class. And then the following week he was able to hold his friends' hands and dance in a circle. That made my day. And some weeks later, I heard Ivan joining his friends in singing *"this little light of mine, I'm gonna let it shine..."*

So, Ivan could finally enjoy participating in music class, at least from time to time. How did I do it? No fancy techniques: I just played video clips for Ivan, danced with him, and clapped with him again and again to the music in the videos. I guess the main thing was to make it fun, and get him used to the physical/tactile activities.

With that said, music class is still a tough subject for Ivan, and I am sure the same is true for many children with autism out there. We need to remember that the whole purpose of music class is to provide additional sensory stimuli not found in regular school activities. I would not sacrifice music class—I believe the additional effort is well justified.

I stand by my interpretation of sensory problems. Children with autism have sensory problems simply because of the powerful but unconnected feedback loops inside their brains. I do not believe that this is an unsolvable problem. By using the modulation technique, we can connect their uncomfortable "Dirac deltas" to positively fun experiences inside their brains, and the sensory problems will either subside or disappear. The multimedia aspect of video clips was what made it fun for Ivan, so video clips still offered the greatest chances of success for learning physical activities. Also, practice makes perfect: I practiced clapping and dancing with Ivan again and again. My main point is, avoidance of stimuli does not seem to me to be the right answer. I instead prefer to try and connect experiences inside their brains through the modulation technique.

Closing the Outer Feedback Loop: Reasoning Skills

As mentioned earlier in the book, neurotypical children develop reasoning skills much earlier than children with autism, simply because neurotypical children are verbal: at the moment of their first speech, they can hear their own voice, and, hence, manage to close their **outer feedback loop**. On the other hand, children with autism are visual. In order for them to close their outer loop and start to develop deep thinking skills, they must first be able to generate their own manual-visual output.

The ability to perform logical reasoning is what separates us from the rest of animals—it is what makes us humans. Unfortunately, for pro-video children, generating manual-visual output is not straightforward. Whereas pro-picture children can simply draw pictures to "close the loop," what can pro-video children do to generate their own motion videos? It is just not realistic to expect young-age children to acquire video-making skills. I struggled for some time with this question, without hitting on a good answer. They say children are our best teachers, and that is very true. In this case, I have learned from Ivan that these children do find an alternative way of generating their own manual-visual output.

When Ivan was four years old, one evening our family went out for dinner. Ivan did something unusual at the restaurant. He was using both of his hands to point towards the general direction of the exit door, and then he moved his fingers as if rearranging objects telekinetically. My wife couldn't make sense out of it. She asked me: "What is Ivan doing?" I then told her: "He is making a movie." And I assured her that that was a good thing: for Ivan has started to close his outer loop.

Around the same time, Ivan's speech also started to improve significantly. Soon we were able to observe a few more curious events with Ivan.

One day in early spring, when the weather was still chilly outside, Ivan stood at the screen door to the backyard. Just as he was about to open the door with one hand, he placed the other hand over and told himself: "Ivan, it is cold outside!" And then, he retracted both hands, and refrained from going to the backyard.

Another day, when he was at the kitchen sink, he was toying with the faucet. And then he said to himself: "Ivan, don't play with water!" And then he stepped down from the chair and walked away from the sink.

In the first episode, Ivan was recalling a comment made by my wife. In the second episode, Ivan was recalling a comment made by Mindy. There are two aspects I would like to point out about these episodes. One, Ivan was viewing himself from a third person's perspective, as is common in children with autism. Two, Ivan was visual. In his mind he was replaying the video memory captured from his daily life experience.

All in all, it was clear that Ivan was starting to develop deep thinking skills. He was reasoning. Not only that, he was becoming more and more verbal.

From Ivan's hand gestures, I could tell that he was generating manual-visual outputs by himself. I asked myself where he acquired his manual-visual output skills from.

My best guess is that it came from the work of my wife. After I told my wife that Ivan's primary communication channel was visual-manual, she purchased some interesting toys, including some elevators, a parking garage and a car wash. She also got all kinds of puzzles and building blocks (foam blocks, "Mega Bloks," etc.). Ivan really enjoyed these toys and often amazed us with the objects he constructed with the building blocks. I told my wife: "You really got some great toys for Ivan." My wife stared at me and proudly replied: "I know my son."

Below is the image of a fairly elaborate "dragon" created by Ivan, when he was four years old.

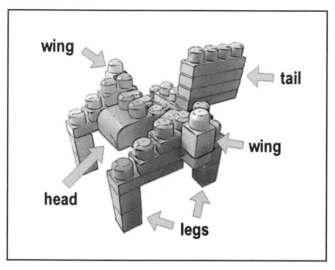

A "dragon" created by Ivan by using building blocks.

Whereas pro-picture children can learn from two-dimensional drawings, pro-video children seem to learn more from three-dimensional objects. I believe playing with building blocks and complex structures such as parking garages, elevators, and car washes helped Ivan to acquire skills in producing his own manual-visual output. Because we have linked his visual inputs (e.g.: elevator and car wash videos from YouTube) to his manual outputs (three-dimensional building blocks and structure-based toys), he was able to close his outer feedback loop and develop deep thinking skills.

To people unfamiliar with pro-video children, it may seem a waste of time to let them watch elevator video clips repeatedly. However, once you understand the visual-manual nature of these children, when you provide the output tools like building blocks for them to express themselves, they will accomplish closing their outer loop and develop deep thinking skills. The verbal route is not the only route to success.

Pro-video children are born different, and they have their own natural way of development.

Creativity: Flipped Flag and "Tickle Bells"

When I was in elementary school in Taiwan, one day we were asked to paint our national flag in our art class. I looked around, and everyone was making the exact same flag. What was the fun in that? Everyone was looking at the flag from the same side. I thought, why not look at the flag from the other side? So I painted the flag as viewed from the back side. At the end of the class, I proudly showed my art creation to my teacher, and his face turned pale. Back then, Taiwan was still under martial law. My teacher admonished me, "Don't ever draw the flag that way," and then he destroyed my art creation and threw it into the trash can. I asked him what I did wrong; he said the flag was flipped. I tried to argue with him that I was simply looking at the flag from the other side. He said, no, the flag was flipped, and don't ever do it again. That was a very traumatic experience. It was only after I grew up that I understood my teacher. He was not worried about me. He was worried about himself. If rumors spread that he was teaching children to draw flipped flags, he would get into serious trouble. I didn't understand freedom of thought back then. When my family landed in Chile, it was still under Pinochet's dictatorship. But to a child like me, it was like fresh air. My mind was finally free to think, free to be creative. Chile lacked political freedom, but that was an adult matter. As far as I was concerned, no one in school told me what to think and how to think anymore. My mind was free at last.

When Ivan was three years old, he learned to sing the "Jingle Bells" song for Christmas. The correct lyrics are:

Jingle bells, jingle bells, jingle all the way.
Oh, what fun it is to ride in a one-horse open sleigh, hey!
Jingle bells, jingle bells, jingle all the way.
Oh, what fun it is to ride in a one-horse open sleigh.

But Ivan's version of the lyrics was:

99

Tickle bells, tickle bells, tickle all the way.
Four-O-Five, Mr. Right: open my suitcase, hey!
Tickle bells, tickle bells, tickle all the way.
Four-O-Five, Mr. Right: open my suitcase.

And we had the best Christmas song, ever. Ivan's ABA therapists loved it, too. So, sometimes, why bother trying to correct our children, when their work is even better than the original?

My point here is, let the children be creative. There is no need to constantly correct their mistakes or quirkiness. We do not want to instill fear in their minds to impede their creativity. Instead, within reasonable limits, we can step back, and enjoy their work, even if things look odd or wrong from our end. Time goes by fast. You may never have another chance to enjoy the fun when your children grow up.

How to Correct Pro-Video Children's Mistakes

Despite the discussion above about letting children be creative, sometime it is necessary to correct children's mistakes. You will have to judge what cases you are willing to let go and what cases you would like to correct. Making changes in pro-video children can be a challenging task. Let me give an example here.

We visited Ivan's uncle's house one day. Ivan was fascinated with one particular hair dryer because its power cord was retractable. However, he was playing with it by manually pushing the power cord back into the hair dryer. His uncle came over and wanted to show him that there was an easier way: simply push a black button, and the power cord would retract automatically. However, Ivan wouldn't let his uncle touch the black button. His uncle thought that it was more fun to use the mechanical button, so he insisted on showing Ivan how it worked. At that moment, Ivan threw a tantrum, and tossed the hair dryer into the air. And everyone around Ivan just had a big laugh. They thought Ivan was so cute. I was in the other room and did not know what the commotion was about, so I came over and asked Ivan's uncle what happened. He showed me one more time and sure enough, Ivan tossed the hair dryer into the air again. Everyone laughed so hard, but I could see the frown on Ivan's face.

UNCLE IVAN	Ivan was pushing the power cord back into the hair dryer by hand. Ivan's uncle attempted to show Ivan that the power cord could be retracted by pushing a black button. Ivan was not happy.
	Ivan threw a tantrum and tossed the hair dryer into the air.

Interrupting a pro-video process causes a tantrum

I let the moment pass, and waited until Ivan was doing something else. Later, his grandpa was showing him the garage, because Ivan liked to take a peek at the garage. At that moment, I brought over the hair dryer, and showed Ivan that if I pushed the black button, the power cord retracted automatically. I did it twice in front of his eyes for him to see.

What happened was that Ivan had an established way of playing with the hair dryer. To him, that whole process could not be divided into its parts, and no part of the process could be modified. It was not amenable to changes. That was why he got annoyed when his uncle tried to push the black button. What I did was two things: First of all, I started a different process. It was me playing with the hair dryer in front of him, instead of him playing with the hair dryer. It was now

101

under my control, not under his control. I was not disrupting his existing process. Second, I modulated the new process into another of his favorite processes—visiting the garage with grandpa.

	I showed Ivan how the black button worked while Ivan was in one of his favorite processes: peeking into the garage with Grandpa.
	Ivan learned to retract the power cord by pushing the black button. Notice the height and upright position of the hair dryer, mimicking the approximate setting of the hair dryer when I held it in front of his eyes.

Correcting a mistake by modulating processes

The next time Ivan went to his uncle's house, I could see him press that black button to retract the power cord. Voilà, success! Success without tantrums. Moreover, from the way Ivan held the hair dryer to push the button, I could tell that he indeed learned from my actions. It was just amazing how much attention he paid to those two little clicks I did in front of his eyes.

The way Ivan held the hair dryer up high was truly shocking to me. I was just amazed at the level of detail that pro-video children could capture. I think the pro-video brain is truly a treasure of the collective human society. These children can view things from angles that no one else can.

Another tricky issue for pro-video children which needs to be corrected is slurring or making mistakes in their speech. A wrong approach would be to try to correct their mistakes in specific spots, like missing words, mistakes in pronunciation, or mistakes in grammar. Pro-video children store entire processes in their brains. To them, it makes no sense to separate a process into its parts. Pro-video children can't focus on specific/isolated spots. Once a process is built and stored inside their brains, it is a done deal for them. You can modulate in additional processes with the existing ones, but it is best not to try to modify specific spots in existing processes. If the child is making a particular mistake, it is best to start with a clean slate, and teach the child to say the correct version in other situations. For instance, earlier I mentioned that I made a honey bear toy from a plastic container to teach Ivan about potty training. Well, the potty training part did not work, but that issue aside, he also could not say "Honey bear goes pee-pee." He would play with the honey bear and say something like, "Anko goes pee-pee." No matter how hard I tried, he never said "honey bear." At most he managed to say "honey goes pee-pee," without the "bear." I realized that he was not going to say "honey bear goes pee-pee," no matter how hard I tried. A different approach was needed. So I started with "Cat: honey cat," followed by "Dog: honey dog" and then "Bear: honey bear." And after that, I taught Ivan to say "Bear, honey bear goes pee-pee." Indeed, whenever I said "Bear," Ivan was able to say "Honey bear goes pee-pee." It took a few months for him to be able to say the sentence without the initial "bear" prompt, but we did get there. I have another example. Ivan learned to answer the question, "How old are you?" by saying "I am three years old." However, he gave the same answer to the question "How are you?" because both questions started with the word "How." In order to teach him to reply correctly, I modified the question to "Hey, how are you?" and he learned to reply with "I am good." Ivan gradually gave the right answer without the initial prompt of "Hey." To ensure that he was able to differentiate these two questions, I made a video clip of a telephone conversation between Ivan and me. Both questions appeared in the video clip with speech bubbles, and Ivan was able to tell which one was which.

Yes, it took Ivan quite a few months before he could say "honey bear goes pee-pee" without the initial "bear" prompt. But that was all right with me. I did not waste time trying to correct him. I simply built a different process for him ("bear, honey bear goes pee-pee"), which functionally worked out all right.

In short, sometimes it is better to fight a tough battle another day, and focus instead on building new processes. The key to new processes is that they should start in a different way from the old process, because pro-video children have a record player inside their brains. If a new process starts out like the old one, the children will replay the entire old process all over again.

I am recapping another piece here: for younger pro-video children, it is best not to try to correct isolated mistakes in their speech or process. Instead, start over with a clean slate, and make sure the new process has a very different starting point from the old one. Pro-video children can't deal with isolated concepts, so it's pointless to try to correct specific mistakes. You may revisit the old process only after the child has completely mastered the new process (or processes). It will take time, but at least during the transition time, you and your child will have a functionally workable solution.

One remaining concern about pro-video children is, will they ever master isolated concepts? The answer is most definitely, yes. Ivan learned to call me Papa, didn't he? Ivan learned to focus on static pictures, right? Doesn't this sound contradictory? Didn't I also say that pro-video children cannot focus on isolated concepts? There is no contradiction. Pro-video children cannot focus on isolated concepts when these concepts are…isolated. When these concepts are connected to something that they are familiar with, something that they enjoy doing, pro-video children can focus and learn. In other words, as long as you give them a solid anchor point, something that they can hold on to, they will be able to learn new concepts. Even though Ivan preferred videos and had his favorite processes, he was able to pay attention to isolated concepts, as long as these concepts were modulated into some main processes that he was interested in. Teaching pro-video children this way may seem painstakingly slow. But let's not forget that these children have their own talents in other directions. Ivan is a keen observer, good with mechanical objects, and a good problem solver. Different children learn things in different ways. They will eventually master everything they need to know—they just need to go about it from different angles. I guess what I want to say is, despite their inability to isolate/extract individual parts of a full process, they are nonetheless capable of absorbing new concepts modulated into an existing process. So insertion seems to work out better than extraction. As for the speed of learning, in Ivan's case, it was actually fast. So no, this is not a painfully slow process. It's more like an autobahn.

I also want to mention that, despite videos being the favorite communication channel for pro-video children, they do learn to communicate using other channels. Pro-video children will learn to focus on pictures/drawings, will learn to read, and eventually will also learn to communicate verbally. The video communication part is an anchor point from which these children can develop other skills. It's a bridge to get these children over to our side, not an oxygen tank that they need to carry for the rest of their lives. I know video editing is time-consuming and requires a lot of work, but better days will soon come. Ivan learned to focus on drawings after just a few videos, and then we could start to draw pictures for him. As a matter of fact, we made a picture diary of his daily activities soon afterwards, so Ivan could be taught with pro-picture techniques that I had successfully applied to Mindy. Ivan soon learned to read simple sentences. And most preciously, Ivan also started to construct new sentences on his own and put them to use, meaning he has was really TALKING! As I have pointed out, with all things considered, the video route is still the fastest highway to success. That's how their brains are wired, that's their native language, and that's how we need to work with them. I think as parents, we owe them at least that much.

Reading Whole Sentences and Stories: Part 1

Ivan's cousin Tin is also a pro-video child. He ran into trouble with reading comprehension. I tried to help him focus on reading. Back then I did not know anything about pro-video children, so the technique I will describe may not be completely ideal, but I thought I might as well mention it here because it did work out alright.

As is typical of pro-video children, Tin couldn't focus on the details of words and letters. He was not good in phonics. He could not parse sentence elements well. When he read a long paragraph, he would slur and skip over many syllables. He also did not have the patience to read a whole story. I immediately knew he needed more visual aids. So we did two things. First, knowing he did not have patience for long stories, we would read them in parts. We would read a few paragraphs, and then let him play a little bit. And then read a few paragraphs more, then let him play again, and so on. Second, I gave him two highlighter pens of different colors, and asked him to alternate highlighting sentence units every couple of words. This way, he learned to break down sentences into smaller units, and familiarize himself with word functions and grammatical structures. He still tried to escape from reading, but he did follow my instructions when I really forced him to sit down and read with me. After familiarizing himself with highlighting sentence units, his reading concentration improved. I wouldn't call it a total success, but his reading did get a whole lot better.

Looking back at it, now I have a whole lot more tools in my arsenal. But anyway, a few things I have learned are:

- Intertwine work and play together, early on in a child's learning process. Don't wait until it's too late. This can be done more easily when the play involves specific objects, such as a bubble blower, a ball, or a model airplane, that you can hold onto until the child finishes a specific milestone.
- Remember to use the picture card album before working and playing with your child. This helps the child know what to expect and what the rules are.
- Use highlighter pens (two different colors) early on, when the child is starting to learn to read individual sentences. And even before that, get the child acquainted with comic book style speech bubbles.
- For children who have not fully transitioned from video memory to picture memory, some video clips may also help.

Reading Whole Sentences and Stories: Part 2

Another technique that I find useful for teaching pro-video children to read is to make them "translate" stories into pictures. Frankly, I myself find it tough to read technical journals, unless I doodle some image representations along the way. I find it even harder to read normal books...my wife has read all the *Harry Potter* books, but to me, that would be a torture. I simply cannot go beyond one or two pages.

Long paragraphs without pictures are just white noise to pro-video children. They don't have anything to hold on to inside their brains. When these children have acquired sufficient drawing skills, by all means please ask them to draw what they are reading. In a sense, let them "translate" words into pictures. This way, they will have something to hold on to inside their brains. It will become more like an "island hopping" exercise: jumping from one picture to the next, instead of drowning hopelessly in the chaotic sea of words. After "translating" enough paragraphs, you can close the book, and ask your children to tell you the story just by looking at the pictures they have drawn.

Here is a specific example that came up while I was helping Tin read *"Junie B. Jones and the Stupid Smelly Bus"* by Barbara Park. Here is an excerpt from the book:

"Mrs. laughed. Except I don't know why. Devil's horns are supposed to be scary."

The main character, Junie B., was wearing a hat with devil's horns. She expected her teacher to be scared, but her teacher instead just laughed. Below is the picture Tin drew. Notice the use of speech bubbles to indicate Junie B.'s thinking process. The larger size girl represents the main character Junie B. The smaller size figure actually represents the nameless Mrs. Teacher.

Translating words into pictures

Finally, modern technology also helps children to read. There are many computer games that make it fun for children to learn to read. I personally have participated in the production of a few educational game titles, in the distant past. Some web-based games that my wife has found useful are starfall.com and tickettoread.com. I mention them simply because our children and/or their cousins have used these sites. There are many more choices out there, so please make some comparison before making your decision.

Teach Them What They Are Good At

I feel terribly sorry for children with autism growing up in our current school environment—particularly for pro-video children. These children are not good in social or group activities. They are not good with their language skills. We impose a curriculum on them that is meant for their typical peers, and we then blame our children with autism for being not good at learning. Sometimes I think we the adults are just masochists: we seem to enjoy inflicting pain on ourselves, at the expense of our children. Why can't parents and teachers accept the fact that these children are not typical but are fine human beings otherwise? Why try to mold these children into a paradigm that is totally foreign to them?

To me, children with autism should instead learn things that resonate more with their inner world, like chess, electronic circuits, advanced math like group theory, complex numbers through geometric algebra, computer languages like Python, productivity applications like Microsoft Excel, video editing software, etc. I built my first crystal radio circuit when I was nine years old, and then I moved on to more complex transmitter/receptor circuits with vacuum tubes and transistors. Children today can do all that at a much earlier age. The problem is, do we have teachers in schools that are capable of teaching this kind of curriculum? We do not. We have teachers who teach our children reading and basic math. We have teachers who teach our children how to be outgoing and popular. These teachers then point their fingers at children with autism and their parents for falling behind in school. For goodness sake, children with autism are some of the brightest minds out there! The problem is not in the children. Children with autism are perfectly capable of shining in calculus, software programming, and video editing. So why aren't we teaching them the skills that they are good at? Some teachers would admit, "Frankly I don't know how to use Excel" or "I have never even heard about the Python programming language" or "What is geometric algebra?" The simple fact is, we don't have the wrong kids—we have the wrong teachers. To be fair, it is not the fault of teachers. The entire special education system needs an overhaul. Special education should not stand for "lesser education"…it needs to be truly special, and go beyond the level of neutotypical education wherever it makes sense.

We keep wasting these children's talents, and then send them to odd/meaningless jobs when they become handicapped as adults. These children are like powerful aircraft carriers, ready to go out and win major battles that challenge humanity today, yet we are using these powerful aircraft carriers as fishing boats; and then we complain that they are too high maintenance, that they are terrible fishing boats.

Masochists: that is what we are. Why do we enjoy creating pain for ourselves? We need to stop imposing a nonsensical curriculum on our children. Instead, we should teach them analytic skills that will make them useful, that will earn them good jobs. Skills that will make them feel good about themselves, skills that will help them contribute to society, and most importantly, skills that will earn them respect from other people.

I probably have screamed enough throughout this book, but let me just say it one more time: we need to stop attempting to make these children typical. Our desire to make these children "normal" causes us to destroy their lives. Please stop this madness. Children with autism don't need to change. It is the adults that need to change and learn to communicate.

4

PRO-PICTURE CHILDREN

Pro-picture children are much easier for me to understand, because I am a pro-picture person. Pro-picture children also exhibit fewer behavioral and language issues. Still, autism is autism, and pro-picture children have autistic manifestations, just like their pro-video peers.

I knew instinctively that I needed to communicate with Mindy through her eyes. So, I started my visual communication with her early on. I remember at one point she wasn't calling out her relatives' names. One of her aunts tried to use high-intensity repetition as a technique to make Mindy say her auntie's name, but it simply was not working. So I stepped in. I made copies of everyone's pictures, then showed the pictures to Mindy, while asking questions like: "Ai đây, ai đây, ai đây? Thảo," or "Ai đây, ai đây, ai đây? Đức," which meant "Who is this, who is this, who is this? (Auntie) Thao," "Who is this, who is this, who is this? (Uncle) Duc." And that was how Mindy learned to say her relatives' names. The picture approach worked pretty well. It only took two days or so for her to be able to say the names of all her uncles and aunties.

When Mindy started to read, I prepared quite a few drawings and taped them on the walls inside our house. I also started to teach her to recognize a few Chinese characters. But at the suggestion of some psychologists and therapists, we did not pursue a multilingual education route. Looking back, I believe that a multilingual environment really wouldn't have made much of a difference for Mindy. I think parents should just do whatever they feel comfortable with.

Pro-video children will develop pro-picture skills at some point. So this chapter is applicable to both pro-picture and pro-video children. However, in early childhood, video clips are the preferred communication channel of pro-video children. So if your pro-video children are not responsive to the picture-aided communication techniques, you may need to go back to the previous chapter.

Character Drawing

To me, character drawing is a very natural thing. I have never taken any real drawing classes besides the art classes I took in elementary school and kindergarten.

happy	sad	tired	mad	really mad
confused	sleeping	ouch!	scared	crying

Facial expressions

I always thought that anybody could draw pictures. But my wife tells me that not everyone can draw pictures naturally. To make things easier, I'll show you some of the typical characters that I draw for my children. I use these characters for picture-aided talking with them on their magnetic drawing board. I have never been ashamed of my kindergarten-grade drawing skills. I have worked with real animation artists in my life, so I know how good they are. But my drawings are made especially for my children, and the professional artists can't beat me on that.

right upwards	upwards	left upwards
right	front	left
right downwards	downwards	left downwards

Facial orientations

Anyway, this book is not about creating artwork. As I have always reassured my wife, there is no right or wrong way when you draw pictures for your children. What matters most is that you are talking to your children and conveying your messages to them. The quality of the drawing is totally secondary. Nobody can replace you: you are your children's parent. Your drawings have special meaning to them. And anyway, the drawings done on the magnetic drawing board are meant to be erased. The characters provided here are just to give you an idea, a starting point. You should let your imagination fly, let your creativity fly, because that is how you can teach your children to be imaginative and creative. You are their role model. Also remember: you love them, and they will love you back.

Another important piece of advice is that you should keep it simple. These visual aids are meant to assist your communication with your children, so they should be easy enough for you to draw very quickly, at the speed of your conversation. Frankly I did not know this style of drawing even has a name: it's called "stick figures." It's an art form as ancient as our prehistoric ancestors.

boy/man	short-haired boy	short-haired girl
long-haired girl/woman	long-haired girl	curly-haired girl/woman

Person characters

I need to point out that the long-haired girl at the bottom center is a character created by Mindy. It's a bit unconventional but I find it really cute and creative.

You may be concerned about how to individualize the characters when you need to include many people in your drawing. That is a needless concern. For instance, my characters for me and for Ivan are identical: I use the boy/man character from the upper-left corner above. I just distinguish the characters by size: I make it bigger to represent me, and smaller to represent Ivan. Also, I often use the same long-haired woman character for both my wife and for our therapists. When Mindy sees two similar characters, she would ask me: "Who is this?" and I would then tell her which one is which. When you have a lot of people, like when you talk about your children's friends from school, you don't need to make all the boys and girls different. You can simply write down their names next to each character, or even just use the initial letters. If your characters are wearing shirts, then you can place the initials on their shirts. Children are smart: they know that the character figures can be recycled to represent different people. So don't worry about individualizing the characters. If the children have siblings, then individualizing might be a good idea, but if they truly look alike, then using initials, or other minor graphical hints, might be enough.

Below is a drawing done by Mindy when she was four years old. Notice the similarity between all the characters and the use of name labels. Notice also the hint from the lengths of hair: Mindy has short hair, others have long hair. The large-sized character "Lara" in the drawing represents an adult. (Mindy's name was edited.)

Mindy and Friends

And finally, I can't emphasize enough the importance of speech bubbles. In Mindy's case, speech bubbles greatly helped her to make conversation, since she actually learned to read before she learned to talk. Young children with autism tend to echo whatever you tell them. The use of speech bubbles helps them to distinguish between other people's speech and their own speech. That is, speech bubbles teach them when it's their turn to speak. Speech bubbles also help the children drop the command word "say," as in "say cheese." Without speech bubbles, Ivan used to include the prompt word "say" when he was echoing.

**An example using of speech bubbles:
Mindy holding a toy syringe**

Picture Diary

For pro-picture children, or pro-video children that have acquired some pro-picture skills, it really helps them to keep a picture diary of their daily routines. The picture diary is a great way to have a conversation with your children. Besides, it's a good reminder for the activities that they need to do. Children may still refuse to sit down for dinner, or to take a bath. That is, they may still protest, but at least showing them the picture diary helps to reduce the chances of tantrums. A picture diary is a way for them to correlate a lot of things: from developing visual attention skills, to cooperating with the daily routine, to developing verbal skills.

Below is an example of Ivan's picture diary.

THE STORY
OF
MY DAY

BY IVAN

EVERY
MORNING

I WAKE UP
EARLY.

THEN I
HAVE MY
BREAKFAST.

THEN
KATIE COMES
TO PLAY
WITH ME.

I AM STILL
DOING MY
POTTY
TRAINING.

PEE PEE

SOMETIMES
I GO TO
SCHOOL.

THEN WE
PICK UP MINDY
AND GO TO
HER SCHOOL.

I TAKE
A NAP.

I PLAY WITH
LINDSAY.

AND MORE POTTY.

PEE PEE

I LIKE TO
PLAY WITH
VACUUM.

WHEN I AM
ALL DONE
WE PUT IT
BACK.

IT'S
DINNER TIME.

117

Ivan's picture diary

Task Album

My wife often tells me that she doesn't know what to draw for Mindy and Ivan, and I would imagine that many parents out there have the same issue. The truth is, every little tiny daily task is an excellent opportunity to teach your children. You may not realize how many steps are involved in some daily routines. You may also not realize how many sentences you speak to your children on a regular basis. Each step of the routine repeats itself, day after day. Prepare a card album for some daily routines, so you can show it to your children, day after day. Your children will pick up the sentences visually and aurally, and that's an excellent way to teach them to read and talk. The task albums work much better than regular children's books because (a) they contain routines that the children are already familiar with, (b) you show the diary to them at the precise moment of their maximum attention for these routines, (c) they contain the exact words of your speech, and (d) they are linked to the most powerful voice—yours. There is no better substitute. Instead of looking around and trying to find ready-made educational materials, I think you should make your own task albums. Besides, the card albums help you bond with your child, which goes a long way towards reducing the frequency and the intensity of tantrums. For pro-video children in the process of acquiring pro-picture skills, you may also consider making video clips out of your card albums. Start with just a few cards or frames, since pro-video children get easily overwhelmed by too many static pictures.

The following is an example of a task album I prepared for Ivan. By this stage he was just over three years old. He could already focus on three to four consecutive pictures and also read quite a few words, so I was pushing him to the next level. You will have to adjust the level of your task album according to your children's pro-picture competencies.

HOW TO TAKE A BATH	PICK A SHIRT.	TAKE IT OFF.	GO TO THE TUB.
SHOWER! HONEY BEAR GOES PEE PEE.	YES, IT WAS FUN.	DRY HAIR.	PUT CETAPHIL. ON MY FACE / ON MY ARMS ON MY TUMMY → ← ON MY BACK ON MY LEGS
WASH YOUR HANDS.	DRY YOUR HANDS.	PUT THE SHIRT ON.	CHANGE DIAPER.

Ivan's task album for taking a bath

Eikona Bridge and ABA

ABA therapists will no doubt find that some parts of Eikona Bridge overlap with the traditional ABA approach, so it is worthwhile to point out some differences. ABA is a general technique to deal with human behaviors. It emphasizes how to change undesirable behaviors, and in that sense I would say it starts off with a negative perspective. ABA is applicable to all human behaviors. It has been applied to employee behavior in a corporate environment, and to other developmental issues, including Down syndrome. Eikona Bridge, on the other hand emphasizes communication, so I would say it starts off with a positive perspective. I do not place much emphasis on behavioral issues, because I believe that most of the behavioral issues are consequences of communication problems. Once the communication problems are resolved, the behavioral issues will go away by themselves. Eikona Bridge also targets autism specifically: the visual approach connects with the natural way of thinking of children with autism, and to their way of understanding the world.

I think Eikona Bridge and ABA can work together. There is no doubt that the intervention of an ABA therapist greatly helps a child's development. ABA is also a scientifically proven technique and has helped countless children with developmental problems, and I am certainly grateful that ABA was there for my children. But as a person on the spectrum myself, I find the current ABA approach a bit too generic, and I think it does not fully resonate with the natural way of learning of children with autism. So my wife and I worked very closely with our children's ABA therapists, advocating for Mindy and Ivan as needed. I would recommend that all parents of children with autism to do the same. ABA is an evolving science, and I hope my findings here can help ABA therapists to better understand the specific needs of children with autism.

Eikona Bridge emphasizes that autism is a communication issue that needs to be addressed, but that does not mean behaviors are ignored completely. I never worried too much about my children's repetitive behaviors. If the repetitive behaviors were there, that was OK; I could use them to teach vital skills to my children. And if the repetitive behaviors disappeared, that was OK, too. Then I taught my children without them. Behaviors were not my focus of attention, communication was.

Among children with autism, Mindy and Ivan are perhaps exceptional when it comes to behavioral problems. One of Mindy's teachers once said, "We can have ten Mindys without problem!" So on one hand I feel like perhaps I am not the best person to offer advice on behavioral problems. On the other hand, I suspect that perhaps we have done things in such a way that our children have avoided many behavioral problems. I will take the risk of being naïve, and share our experience here, based on my latter suspicion.

Communicate Your Intentions through Pictures

Ivan loved to play with our vacuum cleaner. He would pretend to vacuum the floor and hum out a full repertoire of sound effects. After he finished playing, he would move the vacuum cleaner aside but would keep an eye on it. If we tried to put the vacuum cleaner back into the closet, he would throw a tantrum, falling on the floor, crying, and kicking in the air. We knew that we should provide some explanation to him before we stowed the vacuum cleaner away. We tried giving him a verbal explanation. We tried doing it slowly (pretending to put the vacuum cleaner back, then letting him have it again, and then going one step further in the stowing process). But nothing really worked. The situation got so bad that one ABA therapist suggested moving the vacuum cleaner elsewhere and just not letting Ivan play with it anymore. Now I am sure most parents with children with autism have gone through similar situations. But what I am about to tell you next may surprise you.

After Ivan acquired pro-picture skills, that is, to focus and pay attention to static images, I drew the following picture for him on a magnetic drawing board:

Vacuum cleaner in the closet

I explained to him that it was time to clean up and that Papa was going to put the vacuum cleaner back into the closet. When I really did put the vacuum cleaner back into the closet, I was surprised to see that Ivan stayed nice and quiet, as if I'd just done the most natural thing in the world. I said to myself, hmm…perhaps Ivan was tired that night, so maybe he just gave up fighting. A few nights later, my wife told me that she was afraid to put the vacuum cleaner back into the closet and that she thought Ivan was growing too attached to the vacuum cleaner. I told my wife that, first of all, attachment to an object was not a bad thing; it showed that Ivan had passion for certain things, and that it was going to be good for him professionally later in life. Then I drew the vacuum-in-the-closet picture and showed it to Ivan, and he obliged me with the sweetest smile, as if he was telling me that he knew what was coming. Then I stowed the vacuum away, and again, Ivan took it as the most natural thing in the world. So, yes, Ivan understood the message.

I asked myself, was the original tantrum a behavioral issue or a communication issue? Was the fault on the child's side or on the adults' side? Was it the child's behavior that needed to be corrected or was it the adults' behavior that needed correction? I firmly believed that the tantrum must have come from a communication problem, because my picture drawing worked so well with Ivan. I can never forget my surprise when Ivan let me put the vacuum cleaner back without protesting.

The story has a sequel, though. My wife attempted my technique herself the next day, but after she drew the picture of the vacuum cleaner in the closet, Ivan came over to her and erased the picture. And after that, he went back to protesting whenever we wanted to stow the vacuum cleaner away. Frankly I was very disappointed. How come it worked so well until my wife took over, and the picture technique stopped working? I was not able to solve this puzzle at the time, because Ivan was barely three years old, and I was still learning to understand him. Looking back at it today, my best explanation is that my wife has accumulated a negative point in the double-entry ledger inside Ivan's brain, from some previous events, which she did not erase in time. Since that negative point was connected to my wife and not to me, when I drew the picture of the vacuum cleaner in the closet, it worked out all right. However, when my wife drew the picture, the negative entry in the double-entry ledger became connected to the picture drawing, and the technique stopped working. In those early days we were not aware of the mechanism of the double-entry ledger, so we simply never recalled what episode caused a tantrum in the first place, and never managed to cancel it out.

Not all was lost. Repetitive behaviors actually represent the fundamental building blocks in pro-video children's thought processes, and as long as we find a way to participate with the children, we can take advantage of the repetitive behaviors to teach them vital skills. The entire journey may take some time and may include teaching the children to love video clips, helping them focus on drawings and pictures, communicating to them through card albums, introducing reading skills to them, and, finally, closing their outer feedback loop by letting them generate their own manual-visual output. It's a lot of bridges that need to be built, but by stimming, your children have shown you the place to start.

Recap: ALWAYS keep in mind that children with autism are visual, and that your messages need to go through their eyes, not their ears. It is hard for me to see parents talking without visual cues to children with autism. It drives me crazy, because I can see how broken communication is between them. As I have said, without visual cues, you might as well speak in Klingon, because your words are coming through to them as "blah, blah, blah" anyway. For children who already have some pro-picture competence, keeping a card album or a magnetic drawing board handy will help you communicate your intentions. Sometimes when we went out to restaurants, I would just draw or write things on paper napkins, and Ivan would hold on to the paper napkins as if they were some pieces of treasure. For children that are still strictly pro-video, then you have to start with video clips first. You use video clips either to convey a specific message, or to teach your children an initial pro-picture skill, so that they can focus on a card album and magnetic drawing board later. Do not just talk verbally to your children, when they need you to send them visual messages.

Read First—Talking Can Wait

One morning when I drove Mindy to school, she mumbled "cake is sweet" from her car seat. Because of all the noise from the car, because Mindy often still mixed up the pronunciation of the letters *l* and *w*, and because of the lack of context of her sentence, I couldn't make sense of what she was saying. So our conversation went something like:

- "Cake is sweet."
- "Sorry, what did you say, Mindy? Kate is sleek?"
- "No, cake is sweet!"
- "Oh, cake is sue-eat." (I meant to say *sweet*, but in my accent the *w* came out as a vowel.)
- "No, cake is sweet!"
- (Now I was really lost.) "Cake is…sleet? I don't understand you, Mindy…Cake is…what?"

- "Sweet. S-W-E-E-T."
- "Oh, cake is sweet. That's right, Mindy, it is sweet." (Now I made sure I used a consonant for *w*.)

So out of sheer frustration, Mindy spelled the word "sweet" for me! I know, in her mind that was how people spoke: translating visual images of words into spoken sentences. That surely wasn't how typical children would speak.

A few days later, Mindy asked me to turn on the TV for her. I grabbed the remote control and at that moment she said: "I don't like heedimee." Instead of replying with a "huh?" to her, this time I knew better. I asked her: "Would you please spell 'heedimee' for me?" and she said: "Yes. H-D-M-I." I just had to laugh. I told her: "Mindy, you don't need to pronounce it as a word, you can just say 'I don't like H-D-M-I.'" HDMI stood for High-Definition Multimedia Interface. It was a type of device connection. Because our TV was also hooked to a wireless communication device with our computer, sometimes the TV screen showed a panel about the HDMI connection status. That was what Mindy didn't like.

That was our Mindy. She has never been afraid of sounding out new words. Most of the time, she got their pronunciations right. Other times she learned when she was corrected by an adult (especially foreign words, such as "buffet" or "depot"). Mindy learned to talk much later than she learned to read. And the more I think about it, the more I believe that is the right path for children with autism. Yes, Mindy talks perfectly now. But her thinking process remains clearly visual.

Children with autism are visual. Instead of getting frustrated with your children not talking soon enough, try to teach them to read first. For pro-picture children, reading comes naturally: so there is not much to worry about. On the other hand, for pro-video children, the first step is to teach them some pro-picture skills. This is done through weaving static frames into video clips, which was covered in the previous chapter. Only after the pro-video children have become familiarized with static pictures, can you really teach them basic reading skills. Ivan learned to read simple words about three months after I made the first video clip for him. His progress exceeded my expectation. I would have never thought that someone who was not able to focus on cartoon drawings could learn to read so fast. Ivan learned to read longer sentences after he was introduced to Bob Books. These are a collection of very simple books to teach reading to children, with a lot of cool drawings. I highly recommend them.

I can't emphasize enough that reading must happen before talking, especially for pro-video children. Pro-video children are process-based. If they don't have a solid foundation in reading simple two-word expressions and simple sentences, what happens next is that by the time they enter the stage of full sentences (either in reading or in talking), they will slur. By then, making corrections will be exhausting, both for the parents and for the children. Corrections will still be possible if your children are slurring, but it will require much more work and ingenuity from the parents: you will need to come up with processes that have a different beginning from those sentences that the children are already slurring. The longer you wait to do the visual approach, the more cluttered their brains are with slurred sentences, and the less room you have to make corrections.

Mindy talks a lot nowadays and her earlier therapists are all impressed at how verbally proficient she has become. What many of them don't know is that the foundation for Mindy's verbal skills resides on solid reading bedrock.

The following are some examples of early drawings I did for Mindy. I taped these drawings to the wall (using masking tape as makeshift mounting tape, as described in Chapter 2), so that I could show them to Mindy every day. I apologize for the rough drawings and bad handwriting, but I wanted to show at least some original earlier work that I did for Mindy. She was two years old when I made all these drawings. Yes, she was able to read all the sentences in the pictures, despite being largely non-verbal.

The Gorilla is
riding the
elephant !

The cat is
sleeping
by the
fish bowl.

The rabbit
is climbing
the ladder.

What are the animals doing?

As for teaching Ivan to read, I used all the tools I have mentioned earlier: video clips, index cards, and the magnetic drawing board, etc. When Ivan was three years old, he often needed to play with something (e.g., an eraser pen) for his stimming needs. This was especially true when he sat in the high chair, say, to drink milk. While giving him his milk or food, I taught him to read expressions in a sequence like:

> ERASER
> PLAY
> PLAY ERASER
> TO PLAY ERASER
> I WANT
> I WANT TO PLAY
> I WANT TO PLAY ERASER

For someone without pro-picture skills just a few months ago, it was quite an achievement to be able to read a five-word sentence. True reading: word by word, not just memorization of the sentence. I further confirmed that it was true reading two days later. That evening, Ivan came into the bedroom and said: "I want to play sleep." Voilà: that was Ivan's first constructed sentence, ever. It was not perfect, as I knew he meant to say, "I want to sleep." Nonetheless, it showed me proof that he was no longer just labeling, echoing, or memorizing sentences. He was creating new sentences and putting them to use. In short, he was TALKING!

The trick to reading is to take each stimming occurrence as an opportunity for the child to learn. In Ivan's example, I did not fully

128

take away his eraser pen. I just put it behind the bowl of milk, so he knew he would get it back. Then I asked him to read an expression on the magnetic drawing board. I let him stim with the eraser pen again, fed him a few more spoonfuls of milk, and moved on to another expression. He got to drink his milk, play with the eraser pen, and learn to read, all at the same time. The best time to teach your children to read is when they are stimming or doing any kind of repetitive behavior. That's the moment when they are paying the most attention. Do not let those golden opportunities go to waste.

As described earlier, task albums are another good tool for teaching your child to read, because the images are directly related to their daily experience. When your child starts to show boredom with the task albums, that is actually a good sign. That means that your child is now ready for third-party reading material. I guess we missed this clue for a while, until my wife found out about Bob Books by chance. Ivan was totally excited by Bob Books. He would pick up books from the collection on his own, and start sounding out words, even words that he had never seen before. Bob Books contained very simple sentences, and the initial books in the collection had only around twelve pages, each page with one sentence or two. Therefore, children could feel a sense of accomplishment for reading a whole book by themselves. And that was a big motivator to keep them going.

Last but not least, I admit I have been sanguine in using the phrase "read first, talking can wait." to catch your attention. The truth is, very soon after my children learned to read, they gradually started to talk, too. Still, in Ivan's case I observed that his speech did not get much better until his reading got better. In my opinion, for children with autism, reading is the catalyst to talking.

"Hmph!"

One day, just before Mindy turned six years old, I got a one-word text message from my wife. It simply said "**Hmph!**" Hmm...that was strange, I told myself. I replied to my wife asking for clarification on the meaning of "Hmph!" I got the reply: "No you're not!" At that moment I freaked out. I thought my wife's phone had been hacked by someone. But I forgot to ask my wife about it that evening. Instead, Mindy came over to me and asked to play with my phone. And in front of my eyes, I saw her locate the WhatsApp application, open it, type "no, no, no, no thank you!" and send it to my wife. I couldn't believe it. I said to my wife, "I have been getting some weird text messages, did Mindy do all that?" My wife nodded her head and said, "Yes, it was all from your daughter."

The following is an excerpt from Mindy's text messages. (Names are edited. Spacing and grammar mistakes are kept as they were.) Most sentences really did make sense. Some were very heartwarming, and I just had to laugh at her last sentence: "my family were surprised to see Papa texting." It made my day.

```
   Mindy: Hmph!
      Me: what does hmph! mean?
   Mindy: No you 're not.
   . . .
   Mindy: I love dokinchan
   Mindy: Don't  buy anymore  toys save money.
   Mindy: Dad, why are you so sick?
   Mindy: I don't know  why  you're so sick.
           Dad.
   . . .
   Mindy: Dadda. How are you doing  where are
           you now?
      Me: I am in office, now. I am working.
      Me: I am doing fine.
   Mindy: Eeeeeeee moooo••••••••••••
   . . .
My wife: Hehe Mindy goes to sleep with ngoai
           already
      Me: ok, I go swimming... my colleagues
           were surprised to see Mindy texting.
           Till later.
   . . .
   Mindy: Hey! I wanted to see tin & pi!  Ok!
   Mindy: Ok, I go swimming ... My family  were
           surprised to see papa texting till
           later.
```

Excerpt of Mindy's text messages

My wife's phone did not have the "autocomplete" feature, so Mindy actually keyed in every single letter and punctuation mark in her text messages. Not bad for a five-year-old. In case you are wondering, no, she had no help or suggestions from my wife. Mindy created all those sentences on her own.

Children with autism can often communicate better through visual-manual channels than through aural-oral channels. I see too many parents and teachers trying so hard to make their children "normal," while being blind to the talents of these children in the visual-manual direction. These adults might think: "Why teach these children to read first? What's the hurry? Shouldn't we teach them to talk first? Shouldn't we teach them to socialize first?" They do not consider that by going the "normal" route they are harming these children's development. Yes, there are cases of non-verbal children with autism who are fully capable of communicating through writing. You only harm these children by letting them use computers too late, or teaching them to read and write too late. I know many parents have concerns about children using computers or other gadgets too early. They worry about the impact on the children's eyesight, online safety, and children getting hooked to the devices, among other things. I would say, don't prematurely cut off your children's potential communication channels. It is okay to supervise their use of devices, but please do not take a hard stand against technology: we need to explore all possible channels of communication. The important thing is to always remember moderation and modulation, and to use technology as a stepping stone to teach your children other essential life skills.

LIVE Communication

LIVE, as it was introduced at the beginning of this book, is an acronym that rhymes with "five" and stands for:

- **Letters**: Write down your message, and use speech bubbles if necessary. This will help to establish a visual foundation for your children. The sentences will also help your children learn to read. The use of letters also reminds us that for many children with autism, reading comes before talking.

- **Images**: Use pictures and video clips to communicate with your children. Don't just talk. You need to communicate through their eyes, too. Your children are visual.

- **Voice**: Use your voice. This is especially necessary for pro-video children. Your video clips become a powerful tool because it contains the most powerful voice for your children: your voice. Your voice combined with picture drawings form the bridge for your children to become verbal.

- **Experience**: Your drawings should relate to the children's personal experiences, so they have some anchor point to hold on to. This is also why your silly drawings will work out infinitely better than the ready-made materials out there—because your drawings are tailor-made uniquely for your children.

I thank my wife for pointing out the need to summarize the whole message of my book with one singular word. The one thing you need to get out of this book is the *LIVE* communication technique. If nothing else, just remember the *LIVE* acronym. Your children have provided you with a place to stand, and the way you can get into their world and move the earth for them is to communicate with them using the *LIVE* technique. In other words, *LIVE* is your Archimedes' lever!

Slurring

Slurred speech is common in pro-video children. It is a symptom of, likely, a plethora of other issues that need to be addressed. In my mind, slurring is a much more complex problem than behavioral issues. I get more worried about children with autism slurring than about them throwing tantrums. That is also why I have postponed discussing slurring until this point, instead of including this section in the previous chapter on pro-video children. To deal with slurring, you will need virtually all the tools in the arsenal presented in this book, and more.

Even though I think slurring may improve when the child grows older, I believe that dealing with this problem early on can help your child's learning process, social skills, and self-esteem. First of all, slurring tells me there has been neglect. The child needed to acquire some vital skills at an earlier stage, but never fully acquired those skills. I would compare slurring to building a skyscraper one hundred floors high—you cannot wait until completing the very last floor and then complain, "Oops, wouldn't it be nice if we included an elevator in this building, too?" Sure, you could still add an elevator from the outside, but wouldn't it have been better to include an elevator shaft on the inside from day one?

To me, pro-video children slur because they grew up following the typical course of development. They were forced to learn to speak first, and to read later. I think that is the root of the problem. Typical children spend their initial years building up their verbal skills. By the time they learn to read, their progress in reading can be very fast. Reading is like the icing on the cake for typical children, a secondary skill to be built on top of their verbal foundation. In comparison, if children with autism have not been exposed to reading earlier, by the time they learn to read in school they are barely starting to build their visual foundation. Now they are faced with a double burden compared to typical children: the need to struggle with the visual letter patterns, and the need to absorb the aural speech signals. Since pro-video children are process-oriented, they would just store the blurry memory of whatever they could capture from people's speech, and replay the blurry version afterwards, without possibility of change. Making corrections at that point becomes a daunting task for parents and children alike. And, by then, I think there are only two solutions: the first is to let the slurring run its own course, and when the children become older they will be able to solve the problem using their own intellect. This is akin to building the elevator from outside. The second solution is to go back to the basics, and start from the beginning with phonics and visual reading. This is re-building the elevator shaft from inside. Either way, there is no magic pill to solve the problem overnight. You have reached the one-hundredth floor, and it is a little bit too late. Still, later is better than never. Each child needs to build a solid visual reading foundation, so everything mentioned earlier applies. To help your child mitigate slurred speech, here is a list of things to do:

- Make video clips.
- Use a magnetic drawing board and do nightly picture-aided talking using speech bubbles.
- Picture diaries and task albums.
- Teach your child to read when they are stimming or doing repetitive behaviors. Remember to always modulate work into play. Don't just let them play all day long. As long as you modulate work in the right proportion, the children will still have fun and learn at the same time.
- Phonics, especially rhyming words. Pro-video children don't have a problem with initial consonants. What they need to learn is to pay attention to the endings, and realize that similar endings mean similar sounds.
- Sit down and read a book with your child. Bob Books, any story book, or even a comic book. Don't push for too long: mix work with play. And repeat the cycle.
- Act in and record home videos. Do more than one take. Each take should be short. Show them on a computer or TV and ask your child which version is better.
- Detect and write down sentences your child has a problem with. Come up with alternative sentences that start off differently so you can teach your child not to slur with brand-new sentences.
- Educational games for reading skills, either stand-alone or web-based.
- And finally, if self-esteem is an issue, then a children's psychiatrist may be someone to consider working with, as well.

Sign Language

Mindy and Ivan have both had exposure to sign language. Sign language is popular in some ABA circles, too. Our experience with sign language was generally positive. Although sign language never became a significant part of Mindy and Ivan's learning process, it was nonetheless fun and helpful. Even when Ivan was a bit older, when we wanted to give him milk we would still use the sign language for "more milk." Sign language is visual, after all. So my attitude towards recommending sign language for children with autism is, why not?

I think sign language has been less impactful for Mindy and Ivan, because the learning material we purchased was not cartoon-based. I do remember as a young child that I did not like to watch movies or TV programs with real actors. I preferred cartoons. Children with autism prefer simple images: real actors and real background scenes just contain too much additional noise. Still, Mindy and Ivan had a lot of fun with sign language. Best of all, some ABA therapists had various degrees of competency in sign language, so they could also use it as an additional tool to communicate with Mindy and Ivan.

Lining Up Toys

Both pro-picture and pro-video children love to look at symmetric properties. Some like to lean at the edge of a table to observe the straight line running from one corner to another. Some enjoy the process of lining up toys, and get extremely annoyed if the process is interrupted. Again, the absolute worst thing to do is to disrupt their behavior. And the second worst thing is to ignore their behavior and forget to modulate in additional processes to teach your children some vital intellectual skills.

I see no harm in lining up toys. On the contrary, and particularly for pro-video children, lining up toys helps them develop deep thinking skills when they are still not verbal. Tin is good with dominos, and Ivan is good with building complex three-dimensional objects, like castles or car wash facilities. I think pro-video children have an uncanny ability to visualize objects in three dimensions. We just need to make sure they make more and more complex structures: let them use the toy-lining process as a way of expressing themselves. Lining up toys is the first step for pro-video children to generate their own manual-visual output. Later on they can expand their object-building skills to close their "Outer Feedback Loop" as discussed in the previous chapter. It saddens me to see some parents attempting to stop their children from lining up toys, because I see it as interfering with the very seed that will help these children to grow and develop reasoning skills—skills that will ultimately help these children with their speech and socialization.

Selflessness

By selflessness I mean the lack of sense of self, or at least a diminished sense of self. Selflessness in this context does not mean "altruism," although altruism often tends to be one of the manifestations of selflessness.

I would like to share some perspectives as a person with autism growing up into adulthood.

Because people with autism view things through pictures, they have a much lesser understanding of sense of self, and often view things from a third-person perspective. This reminds me of a joke I heard during my undergraduate engineering years. Right after the French revolution, an astronomer, a geologist, and a physicist were sent to the guillotine. The astronomer was the first one up, and when he was asked whether he would like to die face up or face down, the astronomer said he would like to see the sky because that was what he always did, so he chose face up. As the guillotine blade fell, something malfunctioned and the blade got stuck halfway down. Since the execution procedure was legally completed, and the survival of the accused was considered an act of divine providence, the astronomer was let go. Next up was the geologist. He said that since he had worked with the earth his whole life, he would like to die facing down. Once more, the blade malfunctioned and got stuck on the way down. So the geologist was spared, too. Next came the physicist, who didn't have a preference, but chose to die face up anyway. As the executioner was about to release the blade, the physicist screamed in excitement and pointed with his chin: "Wait, wait! I see where the problem is!"

That pretty much sums up the lack of selfishness of people with autism. People with autism are socially inept partially because they have never mastered the skill of manipulation. Instead, they view manipulation as harmful to the larger community. They just view themselves as members of a community. No more, no less, but an equal member of the community. While typical people may be driven by success, personal achievement at the expense of others, or even greed, people with autism would find all that to be nonsense and harmful to the larger community.

(Let me digress. The extreme selflessness of many people with autism does not make them as vulnerable to manipulation by those who would exploit them for personal gain as this joke suggests. Indeed, their goodwill is coupled with an awareness that alerts them to devious behavior. So do not assume that members of the autistic species are easy prey. Instead, respect their lack of guile and do not abuse their goodwill.).

Traits of selflessness can be found early on in children with autism. My nephew Tin loved to dance when he was two years old. The interesting thing was, when he was dancing, he had to make sure everyone in the room danced with him. If someone wasn't participating, he would go over and pull the person into the dance circle. Similarly, whenever we traveled, Mindy would always make sure that everyone wore a seat belt. Ivan often fed me cereal because he knew I liked cereal.

As for me, I remember from my adolescence receiving persistent criticism from my family. They always asked me: "Why do you care so much about other people, instead of your own family?" It was hard for me to distinguish other people from my own family; everyone was a human being. To other people, it was obvious that one should put one's family first. In my case, I had to be taught. You may shake your head all you want. My parents did that, quite a lot. But that's the way I was.

When Mindy was five years old, she was fully verbal, but still had some difficulty distinguishing first- and second-person pronouns. During one evaluation session, her case manager took turns with her playing peek-a-boo, and then asked her questions like: "Can you see me now?" or "Can I see you now?" Mindy got confused all the time. It was like inside her brain there was no direct concept of "I" and "you." These were concepts that she could understand, but they nonetheless needed some "translation" inside her brain, so her response was not immediate. She did not have reflexes for answering "I" and "you" questions. She needed to think about them. At home, I repeated the same game with Mindy, but this time using third-person questions like: "Can Mindy see Papa now?" or "Can Papa see Mindy now?" and indeed she did not have a problem answering the questions.

Mindy started to read *Calvin and Hobbes* early on, when she was around three years old. What made this series so special and different from other comic books was that it toggles between first-person and third-person's perspective. The tiger came to life when the picture frame was viewed from Calvin's perspective, but turned into a lifeless stuffed animal when viewed from third-person perspective. Also, when Calvin was imagining that he was a space explorer, you would see him turn into Spaceman Spiff, while in reality he might just be sitting in a boring classroom. My sister, to whom I'd sent a copy of the book years before when she had her first child, just could not understand it. She asked me, "Why does the tiger change shape now and then?" Oh boy. The interesting thing was that when Mindy started to read *Calvin and Hobbes*, she had absolutely no problem understanding the change of perspective. *Calvin and Hobbes* captured the way pro-picture people think and view the world very well.

So there you go. Mindy, being autistic, had problems understanding "you" and "I" questions, but had no problem understanding *Calvin and Hobbes*. My sister, of course, had no issues with "you" and "I" pronouns, but had a hard time understanding *Calvin and Hobbes*.

The selflessness of people with autism is not just inferred from casual observation. There has been some scientific study that supports the selflessness character of high-functioning autistic people. In 2008, Dr. P. Read Montague Jr., Dr. Pearl Chiu, and a team from Baylor College of Medicine performed a study of high-functioning autistic adolescents by scanning the subjects' brains using functional magnetic resonance imaging (fMRI), and they then compared the results to those of typical people. They found a difference in activity in the cingulate cortex for the "self" response: it was significantly less for the autistic group. In simpler words, the subjects in the autistic group showed poor recognition of self.

For younger children, the autistic selflessness points to the need to treat these children very differently from their typical peers. Children with autism are not guided by personal greed and are certainly not manipulative, so parents and teachers need to relax their fear that stems from: "If we don't manipulate the children, the children will manipulate us." Because of this characteristic of selflessness in children with autism, parents should perhaps be more generous towards the demands of children with autism: unlike typical children, children with autism do not demand things for demand's sake, and they are less likely to get into the habit of manipulation. Because children with autism view themselves from the third-person perspective, when they make demands they are more likely to have factored in other people's concerns (if that's not the case, you can explain those specific circumstances to them), so their demands often tend to be quite reasonable. I don't mean to say that parents need to always fulfill the demands of children with autism, but I am just saying that in relative terms, parents need to be more generous, because children with autism: (a) tend to make fewer demands, (b) their demands tend to be reasonable, and (c) it is less likely that they will become as manipulative as typical children when their demands are constantly fulfilled.

For older children with autism, parents should keep in mind that these children tend to be selfless and view things from a third-person perspective. At times this may be frustrating for parents, since children with autism tend to look at things in black and white, and they will not come to your defense when they find that you are the one at fault. I would say most of the conflicts with adults with autism result from this characteristic. People with autism tend to look at the greater good of the whole community. It is not like they are saints or anything like that; it is simply that they have a lesser sense of self, and a lesser need for an identity. That may get them into trouble easily with family, in some cultural groups, in school, and at work, where blind loyalty is commonly expected. I will not suggest "solutions" for teenage or adult people with autism, as this topic would wander into political territory, be it family politics, ethnicity politics, classroom politics, or workplace politics. Different people have different values and different opinions, and that is okay. But I just want parents to be aware of their children's characteristics. The better that people understand autism, and when more people judge things objectively, based on what they know, the better things will be for everyone.

Remind Them That You Are a Friend

Mindy sometimes learned bad habits from TV or school, like pretending to get mad, yelling, and hitting or punching us. That drove my wife crazy. Frankly, I was totally incapable of disciplining my daughter. It was a weakness on my part. What I usually did was to ask Mindy, "Mindy, is Papa your friend? Didn't Papa give you food samples in Costco today? Didn't Papa give you cheese today? Doesn't Papa take you to school every morning?" And Mindy would nod her head in agreement. Then I'd follow with, "So, why did you hit Papa? You shouldn't hit Papa, OK?" And to defend my wife, I would remind Mindy, "Mindy, isn't Mami your friend? Doesn't Mami make dinner for you every night? How long do you think it takes to make dinner? Didn't you make soup in school the other day? How long did it take you? About one hour? And Mami has to make dinner for you every evening. That's a lot of work, Mindy. See? Mami is your friend, and you shouldn't hit Mami." And usually that would be the end of it, and she would give my wife a kiss. If it is too hard to deal with your child at a given moment, then wait until later for a better moment, like when you are giving something good to your child (e.g., a cookie or ice cream). At that moment, you can ask again, "See, Mommy gives you a cookie. So, is Mommy your friend?" And in the future you can refer back to the cookie event. To me, children are equal-rights human beings. I find the use of authority to be counterproductive, especially when dealing with children with autism. A better route is to treat them as equals, and remind them that you are a friend.

Behavioral Problems: Lion or Lamb?

During one of our regular visits to see Mindy and Ivan's uncle, this is what happened. The kitchen and the family room had just been remodeled, and the furniture was still not in. So Ivan was able to ride a tricycle in that big area inside the house. There was a glass sliding door leading to the backyard, and I was afraid that Ivan would hit the door and break the glass. At one point, Ivan was actually hitting the frame of the door with the tricycle, and I screamed out a deafening "NO!" I guess everyone jumped when I screamed. I have taught lectures as a teaching assistant to over 150 students in auditorium-size rooms, so I knew how to be loud. After that "NO," I guided Ivan to ride his tricycle away from the sliding door. That evening my wife told me that Ivan's Grandpa was very impressed that I screamed so loud at Ivan, yet Ivan did not cry at all. She said that although she and Grandpa were also very close to Ivan, if they did the same thing, Ivan would have surely thrown himself on the floor kicking and crying. When Grandpa asked my wife why Ivan did not cry, my wife just told him, "They are from the same species, they understand each other."

"Tricycle, door, no, no, no"
Picture communication prevents tantrum

Well, that was what everyone else saw: me screaming at Ivan, and Ivan learning to ride away from the glass sliding door, as easy as that. What they did not see was the groundwork I laid out ahead of time. When I first saw the danger, I drew a picture for Ivan using the magnetic drawing board. (We always traveled with a magnetic drawing board, because it was the communication device we used most with our children.) I already did the work explaining the danger to Ivan, visually. By the time he was mischievously hitting the glass door, he actually already knew he shouldn't do that. He was just making sure his interpretation of my message was correct, and was trying to see if he could push the boundary a little bit. In short, our communication didn't just happen verbally when I screamed "NO!" at him. Our communication happened much earlier, and it was visual, not verbal. When I screamed, it was a surprise to everyone else, but not to Ivan. No surprise, hence no tantrum. Best of all, I knew I could let him ride the tricycle safely now. He had verified his understanding of my message. Even a few days after we went back home, he would still smile and mumble "tricycle, door, no, no, no," because that was what I drew on the magnetic drawing board.

My mother once said that I was usually so well behaved, as mild as a little lamb, but when I got mad I turned into a big monster, as ferocious as a lion. So I guess I must have also thrown tantrums, even into my teens, perhaps even into adulthood.

It's easy to dismiss tantrums of children with autism as a behavioral problem. However, I would argue that is an inaccurate approach. I would like to offer my perspective here, so that we can figure out a way to resolve conflicts with children with autism.

First, children with autism are not typical children. They are not driven by personal greed. They tend to be selfless and view things from a third-person point of view. They view themselves as equal-rights human beings. They do not have the "me first" reflex of typical children.

This immediately renders some common sense approaches useless. In particular, parents should never attempt to come in from an angle of authority, for this immediately and permanently causes disruption in your relationship with your children. You lose respect immediately and permanently in the eyes of your children with autism. You need to approach your children with autism as equals. And you need to forgo all attempts to manipulate and to use sugar-coated lies. This is probably easier to accept in Western culture, but in Eastern culture where obedience and submission is commonly expected, children with autism can more easily run into trouble.

Second, I remember most of the times I exploded I did so because I could see what was coming. It was like I was telling the whole world "don't do it, don't do it" and people did it anyway. Contrary to common perception, children with autism do not just explode for no reason. Inside their minds they have been telling the world what should be done or what should not be done, but no one listened. In all fairness, the opinions of children with autism were never fully communicated to the outside world. So the outside world often becomes shocked at these children's behaviors. The outside world views those behaviors as uncalled for, as unexpected, as surprising. I view it as a communication problem. Of course when children with autism grow up, they must learn to better communicate their feelings, their opinions, and where they stand on issues. But while they are still young, particularly when they still cannot communicate verbally, the responsibility of communicating falls to the parents.

In real-life situations, communication is not always easy. Picture drawing is not always feasible. Most of the time this infeasibility is a result of time limitation—some matters need to be resolved right away, so there is no time for further communication. Unfortunately, this haste often translates into tantrums by the children. What can be done in these cases, when picture-aided communication is not practical? What if a tantrum has already happened?

When a tantrum happens, let it subside first. Then spend time with your child afterwards, perhaps before going to bed, and figure out the cause of the tantrum. Find out what bothered your child. Use pictures with arrows or lines, offer a list of possible causes of the explosion, and ask the child to help you identify the precise cause of the tantrum. Children develop frustration differently with different people. In Ivan's case, at one point he associates his frustration more readily with my wife than with me. Still, picture-aided talking always helps to reduce the degree of frustration. It helps to calm children down. It helps them to reason. Allocate time to do picture-aided talking with your children on a regular basis. Find out about their daily life, how they are doing in school, what bothers them, and why they threw the tantrum the last time. Explore and understand their vision of the world, offer your perspective, and discuss the pros and cons of your children's perspectives with them, and help them to understand which perspectives would bring the most good to everyone. I need to emphasize that children with autism have long memories for bad experiences, not in the remembering the details, but in the remembering that they have had a bad experience. The negative feeling or resentment is cumulative. It is as if they keep an accountant's **double-entry ledger** inside their brains. For each instance that goes unresolved, you will accumulate a negative point. You really need to address and explain your perspective as soon as possible, and don't let the resentment build up, day after day, month after month, and year after year. You have no right to complain about your children's increasingly annoying behavior if you have never taken the time to properly talk to them, in their language. Use pictures in all your discussions. Your children will appreciate you for talking in their language. Picture-aided talking immediately brings you closer to their inner world. Using the pictures and "speech bubbles," you can also teach your children to verbalize their displeasure/dissent.

Here is a concrete example how I was able to remove Ivan's tantrum. At one point, Ivan was not having many tantrums and was very easygoing. One day my wife told me that lately it was hard to get Ivan into the high chair for dinner. I thought that type of tantrum was already gone, but obviously it made a comeback. I tried to get Ivan to sit down for dinner myself, and indeed, he threw a tantrum. Instead of asking my wife what Ivan was doing right before the dinner, I asked her point-blank: "Did you lie to him recently?" and my wife replied: "Yeah, I think I did."

Well, it turned out that it was not precisely a lie. It was one of the earlier days of Ivan going to a new school in the afternoon, and what happened was Ivan took a nap at school and when he woke up he did not see my wife. My wife was actually still in the school, but just not in the classroom. Ivan felt like my wife played a trick on him, and cried very hard. So I told my wife that the dinnertime tantrum probably had nothing to do with dinnertime itself, and that what happened was that my wife just accumulated a negative point in Ivan's double-entry ledger inside his brain. The way to remove that negative entry was to do picture-aided talking with Ivan.

So we did two things. One, at night I drew pictures on the magnetic drawing board to Ivan, in my wife's presence, and explained to Ivan that Mommy had other things to do, but that Mommy would come back to pick him up later in the afternoon. I also drew pictures to tell him that when he woke up, he would play with the teachers, go out to the playground, and then have a class. The second thing my wife did was to show him a task album about these same points whenever she dropped Ivan off at school. In just two days or so, we saw the dinnertime tantrum disappear. So, sometimes, if you just focus on the immediate events of a tantrum, you may be missing the point. Children with autism have long memories and do keep a double-entry ledger inside their brains. You may have accumulated the negative point from an earlier incident, so you may need go back and cancel that precise entry, using proper picture-aided talking.

Again, I strongly believe that most tantrums are not behavioral problems *per se*: they usually originate from a communication problem. Having time to draw pictures to show your child would reduce a lot of these behavioral outbursts. Your children may not fully understand your justification in pictures, but they will appreciate your effort in trying to explain it to them. Once you solve the communication problem, the behavioral problem will go away.

One last thing: try to avoid justifying your actions by saying they are just the rules. You need to go one step beyond that. You need to explain the motive and purpose of your actions. Rules just won't cut it, because they do not treat children with autism as equals. Rules come from an angle of authority, which is the wrong approach for children with autism. If you need to set up rules, you need to explain to your children the rationale behind the rules and the benefits of having them.

A Busy Mind

When I was a little boy, I used to wear a frown during my sleep. My mother told me, she always wondered what I was thinking. She said, I looked like I was thinking about some important matters. Well, I guess nothing was that important when you were a child. But she was right in observing that my mind was always busy, even during my sleep.

In my adult life, my mind is still always busy. Very often, I get into a "trance" mode, reflecting about issues or problems. I think most people with autism share the same characteristic. They are either busy fulfilling a recent request, or trying to solve other longer-term problems. To outsiders, it is often hard for people to realize how busy the mind of a person with autism is. Very often people tend to assume that if any person is quiet, then the person must be free. With the autistic species, this assumption tends to be a very bad assumption. If a person with autism is already busy handling two or three trains of thought, and an outsider bursts in with additional requests, then the situation could simply become too overwhelming.

I do not believe that it is entirely accurate to describe people with autism as incapable of multi-tasking. With familiarization, I believe they can multi-task as well as typical people for daily tasks, and they can even forgo perfectionism for increased productivity. However, it does take time for people with autism to transit from the "trance" mode to the "multi-tasking" mode. Human brains have limited amount of energy: our thought processes could either go deep or go wide, but not in both dimensions at the same time.

Advanced notice goes a long way towards reducing the likelihood of tantrums in children with autism. Instead of telling your children: "Time's up, clean up!", it is often much better to tell them: "OK, you have 3 more minutes, and then you'll have to clean up." As for adults with autism, it usually helps to ask first questions like "Are you free now?" "Is this a good time?" before getting into the issues that you want to discuss with them. In short, please remember that the autistic mind is a busy mind.

Another Type of Repetition

Once upon a time, while my in-laws were visiting, I was translating a song from Chinese to English, as a hobby. I did not like any of the existing translations done by other people, so I thought I might as well come up with my own version. I would play the song over and over again, sing along, make corrections, and then try again. Needless to say, it drove my mother-in-law nuts.

It was not repetition for the sake of repetition. In each iteration, I was paying attention to specific spots. Then I made those spots better, only to discover that some other spots also needed more work and the process went on over and over again. A casual observer would not sense the fine differences, and might think that I was simply crazy, listening to the same song over and over again. This type of repetition is different from the typical repetitive behaviors of people with autism. I would call it P & P, for "planned and purposeful." So we have two types of repetition:

- Stimming: people with autism often cannot explain why they do it, or would provide a very vague rationale.
- P & P: they can explain very clearly what they want to achieve in each iteration. They are exploring alternatives and they want to make things perfect.

So pay attention to your children's repetitive behaviors. If they are simply repeating the same activity (stimming), then that would be a good anchor point upon which you can teach your children new skills. But if your children are repeating something to achieve perfection (P & P), that would be a good sign, as long as they don't use up all their time to do just one single activity. Striving to be perfect is not a bad thing, as long as the children also acquire some time management skills, which could be as simple as learning to set an alarm clock (or to keep a to-do list in the case of older children). P & P is the very skill that scientists use for doing research. Though P & P is different from stimming, the two types of behavior are related.

Lonesomeness vs. Loneliness

This is one of the misconceptions that many people have about people with autism: equating lonesomeness with loneliness. Just because children/adults with autism can handle lonesomeness, it doesn't mean that they can handle loneliness. People with autism may like lonesomeness from time to time, but they surely don't like loneliness. I can't stress enough the need that people with autism have to be surrounded by others. As many researchers have pointed out, it's not the number of friends that matters; it's the quality of friends that matters. (See for instance N. Bauminger and C. Kasari's article "Loneliness and Friendship in High-Functioning Children with Autism," in *Child Development*, volume 71, year 2000.) Like all other children, children with autism cannot be left alone, period.

I can illustrate the case with my own experience. During my high school and college days, I went to parties thrown by my friends. I would get there, only to find out that I did not like the dancing, the soda drinking, or the group chat. A friend who hosted a party once got worried that I was not doing anything, so he kindly offered me a book to read. The idea was quickly shut down by my other friends: no, they said, no one reads a book at a party! So they took the book away and luckily I never became labeled as "the guy who read a book at a party." I was labeled with something else later, though. That was in my graduate school years. Yes, even PhD students in science would throw parties now and then. I became known as "the guy who slept in the closet at a party." Yes, that did happen. I was not good at socializing, and did not want to embarrass my friends by napping on their beds, so I hid myself in the closet to take a brief nap, and unfortunately I was caught. The thing was, while I didn't like the social activities, I surely enjoyed being around people. I did not like the dancing, but I surely enjoyed listening to music. And when some of my closer friends were not busy socializing with others, I did enjoy chatting in a smaller group of familiar faces. Because I was among friends, I was not ridiculed for my closet episode. In science, people get used to eccentric characters. Eccentricity was not the exception: it was the rule. So no one made a big deal out of my oddness.

Children with autism should be encouraged to participate in social activities. Yes, your child may even sleep in the closet at a party, but so what? They are human beings and need to be around people. Just look at it this way: they'll have a good time, and they'll get some real-life stories to tell their grandchildren. You can't beat that.

Self-Injury

When Mindy was diagnosed with autism, I immediately called my parents and asked them whether any of our relatives had autism or speech delay. It turned out that I did have a niece on my father's side that had speech delay. But my Mom told me that the girl received some help and was fully verbal now. Taking into account that our extended family spanned three continents, it was tough to collect my relatives' histories. I hadn't seen most of them in decades, and many of them I had never even met. I later told my Mom that, according to all the descriptions I have read, I had autism, too. She immediately went into denial mode. She said I never had speech delay, so I could not possibly be autistic.

But my sister knew better. She was the only witness to something horrible that no one else in the family saw: I used to bang my head against the wall, in private. I was probably seven or eight years old. I don't remember exactly why I felt frustrated. I do, however, remember to this day the purpose of banging my head: I wanted to kill myself.

It seems I did not bang my head hard enough, for later I still got a PhD in theoretical physics. But the scary part of this story was that my parents were oblivious to the suffering of their child. I clearly felt like I had no one to communicate with. People around me were totally unaware. Even after my sister reported what she saw to my Mom, no one truly understood the severity of the incident.

I was surrounded by people, yet no one was communicating on my frequency. Autism, to me, is first and foremost a communication problem. Parents are so busy today that they may not spend enough time trying to understand their children, and may not know how to view things from a child's perspective.

Don't get me wrong, I love my parents. But I wish what happened to me would never happen again to other children. Today we have some clues about how to communicate with children with autism. Back then, people did not know anything about this condition, and in my particular environment, they did not even have a name for it.

Don't wait until self-injury happens. Communicate with your children early on. Talk to your children through pictures and videos. They will appreciate it. If your children are already causing self-injury, work hard to communicate with them and please don't give up: better late than never. I have already mentioned all the rules. Do not attempt to interrupt their established processes—make videos to teach them additional skills and to set expectations for new activities, prepare card albums, draw pictures and use picture-aided talks (this might be harder for pro-video children at the beginning, but it works great after the children have acquired pro-picture skills), participate in their repetitive behaviors, and modulate in additional skill-teaching activities.

Accident Prevention Drills

When children climb or step on an unstable structure, or play with objects in a dangerous way, accidents can happen. If a situation is dangerous for typical children, it's likely to be even more dangerous for children with autism. Sometimes this because of these children's lesser awareness of the environment, sometimes it is because of their peculiar interests, and sometimes it is because of their persistent repetitive behaviors. Accidents happen more easily for children with autism. Given the accident-prone nature of these children, accident-prevention drills become especially important.

With Mindy, I could either scream a little bit, make a "simulated fall" with her with her head gently touching the floor, or draw a picture, and she would understand. One has to be careful with the "simulated fall" technique, though, since children may find it entertaining. A more serious tone is needed. If a particular child misinterprets a drill as a game, I'd say the drill should be avoided.

Accident prevention was not as easy with Ivan, and we had to change our strategy several times. At the beginning, we yelled whenever Ivan was standing in a precarious setting. But Ivan cried much more easily than Mindy, so that didn't work out too well. Also, back then Ivan still did not understand pictures, so that left "simulated fall" as the next choice. The problem was, Ivan also got discouraged from the "simulated fall" and ended up crying all the same, because he sensed that he was being lectured. Finally I realized that if I did the simulated fall myself and made him watch me fall, hit my head, and cry, he would pay attention and get the message without throwing a tantrum.

Accident prevention picture

So we do have choices, ranging from verbal admonishment, picture/video demonstration, simulated accident on the child, or simulated accident by adults. Choose whatever method can help your child understand the danger involved. Prevention is always better than dealing with the outcomes of an accident.

Simulation also helps greatly with preventing children from getting lost in a big crowd. Both Mindy and Ivan could easily get distracted in supermarkets, warehouse stores, or entertainment parks. So on a few occasions I would turn quickly into an aisle or some other hiding place, and would then peek through discrete openings to see their reaction. Of course, they would panic when they realized they were alone, but I would appear immediately to calm them down. After a few times they learned to check on me and/or my wife on a constant basis, and they also learned to stay close to us.

Discipline

When I was younger, I had a laughing problem. My laughs were loud and strange. I especially couldn't handle watching comedic movies, movies where the characters made embarrassing mistakes. I got embarrassed very easily. More than once, my laughing got me into trouble. On one occasion, while I was in graduate school, I went with my classmates to pick up some lunch at a small family-run takeout food place. I cannot remember what my friends told me, but it was something funny, and I laughed heartily. The owner at the fast food place was so busy that he mistook my laughing as mockery of him, and essentially kicked me out of the store. To me his reaction was so out of the blue, and all my friends felt sorry for me. We were talking about some funny situations totally unrelated to the store, but the lunch line was busy and it was simply not the place for explanations or arguments. I was so mad that I boycotted the place for the rest of my stay at the graduate school.

On another occasion, I was playing ping-pong with another graduate student, and my roommate was watching the game. At some point someone said something funny, and I started laughing. Then, my opponent started to mock me. I was so busy hitting the ping-pong ball that I did not even realize I was being mocked. My roommate was nice and jumped in to help me out; he told the other student: "You probably find Jason's laughing unnatural, right? But that's just his way of laughing. He always laughs that way."

Where am I going with this story? My point is, the signals inside children with autism are amplified. In many of these children, the intensity of their feelings and emotions could be overwhelming. I was really bad at handling embarrassment. Even just watching characters in a movie being embarrassed would make me feel the same embarrassment, but amplified. And when I felt something was funny, my laughing would become uncontrollable. For my family and close friends, my behavior was just me being myself. For strangers, well…let's just say that I could get into trouble. Back then I did not know I was autistic. Now I understand that I behave the way I behave, because signals inside my brain are simply amplified.

Now let's address the subject of discipline. Children are children, whether they are autistic or not. And occasionally some disciplinary actions are unavoidable. However, special care must be taken when administering disciplinary action to children with autism, for any minor actions may cause intense feelings and emotions for these children. We do not want to cause permanent damage.

Not all children with autism react with the same intensity to punishment. (Yes, I know, I should say "disciplinary action" instead of "punishment," but simply changing the words won't make us better parents.) It is a trial and error process. Something as mild as a time-out may not be a big deal for some children, but could be very detrimental for others.

As mentioned in the pro-video chapter of the book, it is necessary to do some picture-talking after handling a situation with your children whenever there is an adverse reaction. You cannot afford to accumulate negative points in the double-entry ledger in their brains. You need to cancel out the negative events. As I have repeatedly mentioned, even if these children are non-verbal you need to talk to them through picture drawings about what they did wrong, why they were punished, what they should do in the future; and then give them a hug, a kiss, or a high five at the end.

As for time-out, it is usually a good course of action, both at home and in school. But if you observe that your children have adverse reactions to public humiliation, I'll pass along a piece of advice: give the children a piece of paper and a pen (if they can draw pictures already), and tell them that they can draw pictures if they want to. Tell them they can draw anything they like. I read about this technique from a passage in the book *Nobody Nowhere: the Extraordinary Autobiography of an Autistic Girl*, by Donna Williams, where she described her growing up as a child with autism. It totally made sense to me. The picture-drawing-style time-out still serves its "punishment" purpose, as it deprives the children from their primary activities. However, it will divert the attention of the children away from dwelling on events that caused the punishment in the first place. For children that are overly sensitive to embarrassment and humiliation, they have already gotten the message with the time-out, and there is really no need to let their brains dwell on those events. For these children, low-intensity gentle reminders work better than single-time strong punishments.

Montessori Schools

Montessori schools emphasize visual and sensorial development. Montessori schools are also characterized by mixed grade classrooms. This is particularly helpful for students with developmental issues, as they can progress to the next grade without formally repeating the previous grade.

This structure means that Montessori schools would be ideal for children with autism, right? Unfortunately, the situation is a little bit more complicated. Though Dr. Maria Montessori's teaching methods certainly are well suited to children with autism, and as a matter of fact she worked extensively with children with developmental problems, today's Montessori schools are geared towards mainstream children, and Montessori teachers are not usually trained to work with children with autism. As a result, children with autism can easily be neglected in the Montessori environment.

All of this is quite unfortunate. To me, the Montessori Method and autism special education are supposed to be the very same thing. Yet, currently the gap in understanding between the two communities is just too wide to repair with any ease. Autism educators tend to be aghast at children with autism being left alone and being deprived of more social interaction, and Montessori teachers may view these children as additional burden, since today's Montessori classroom is supposed to be a practical life environment where children help out with the running of the program.

Because most Montessori schools are still on the learning curve with handling children with autism, I would suggest that parents be careful. First, find out the school's track record with children with autism. If the school is inexperienced with children with autism, shadowing may be a good idea, especially in crowded classrooms. The presence of an outside adult can help prevent or defuse potentially tense situations. Open-school policy is definitely a plus. In my children's school, parents can drop by anytime and even work with the children during class time. I know not all schools share the same open-school policy, and we have been truly grateful and lucky to have found such a school. Do as we did: check around with a few different schools and find out your best choice. From my Google search in these last few years, I have noticed an increase in people advocating for Montessori-style education for children with autism. At the same time, more schools are becoming familiar with children with special-needs. I even see teaching techniques improving in public schools, for children with autism.

I think I would have enjoyed the Montessori environment myself. When I was in high school, I liked to sneak into the physics lab and play with experimental devices. I also enjoyed sitting alone on the second floor balcony, dangling my legs in the air, and thinking about life. Having personal time and space, while knowing friends were only a few feet away, and having an opportunity to develop close friendships with a small number of peers was the ideal environment for me. My kindergarten and elementary school were normal-style public schools, and I did not have particularly fond memories of them. But my high school was different: I lived at a boarding school. (It was not a fancy one. As a matter of fact, it was run by the government, mostly for smart but underprivileged children throughout the country. Very often they fed us horse meat—I kid you not—and we took cold water showers in sub-freezing temperatures. Oh, and the bathrooms had no doors...should I stop? The school did produce a President of the Republic, so it was not that bad.) I really appreciated the individual time and space I had inside the school, so I know that individual time and space to explore, discover, and think is an important component in the education of children with autism. This is not at the expense of social interaction; I also liked to join group activities. But I think that my elementary school and kindergarten weren't as good because I did not have the personal time and space for inner development.

So my take is that Montessori is worth trying, as long as additional attention is paid to the school's experience with children with autism. An aide would be a great asset. I know the Montessori Method is great for visual-sensorial development, but from my perspective as a person with autism, I value Montessori's emphasis on individualized development even more. If your children go to regular public schools, be sure to create personal time and space for them to do some exploration on their own, either as part of school activities or outside of school.

Teach Your Children to Defend Themselves

One of the hardest things to do as a parent is to teach your children to say no to you. As paradoxical as it may sound, this job is what parenting is all about, especially in the case of children with autism. Teaching them to say no and to protest will show your children that you care about them, and that you love them. And wonderful things can happen, because one day when you least expect it you will find out that they do reciprocate and care about you.

Children really need to learn verbal skills to protest and to defend themselves. Start at the very least with "no" and "I don't like it." Screaming at you is a valid response. (Yes, there are children that would rather take things in stride than let out a scream.) These are essential skills not only at home, but also in school and other settings. I would rather see my children be able to vent their frustration, than see them be abused by others at school, including by adults. We need to give our children tools to fight back and to defend themselves, so that they can be emotionally strong and not be abused psychologically. If you want your children to be able to defend themselves against others, then start by teaching them to defend themselves against you.

Frustration of a High-Speed CPU

One common misconception out there is that children with autism are intellectually disabled. Nothing could be further from the truth. In fact, most children with autism show great talent in certain focused areas.

In fact, it would be safer to assume that children with autism process information at such a high speed that they develop behavioral problems because their external communication skills simply cannot catch up. Do not assume that children with autism are unable to understand people's emotions, or unable to analyze and solve problems. Children with autism often feel frustrated because they can see things several steps ahead of time and in multiple dimensions. What typical people consider fun or important may appear trivial and boring to children with autism. Because children with autism are generally unable or unwilling slow down to the speed of typical people, they develop frustration easily.

Children with autism usually cannot verbalize their feelings, which are often expressed instead as behavioral problems, not because they want to cause trouble but because they feel misunderstood. They are smart, and their brains sometimes work faster than what typical people are able to analyze and comprehend.

When I started to devote more of my time to Ivan, I did not have as much time for Mindy. When Ivan started to understand my drawings, I spent more time drawing pictures on the magnetic drawing board for him. One day I grabbed the magnetic drawing board to draw some pictures for Ivan. When Mindy saw me do that, she just started to sob. I was confused; I asked her whether she was crying because:

- She did not like me using the drawing board to draw pictures for Ivan.
- She wanted me to draw pictures for her.
- She wanted me to spend time and play with her.
- She was bored and wanted Mami to play with her.

She shook her head at each of the explanations. I explained to her that I needed to spend time with Ivan to draw pictures for him. I asked her whether that was OK and she nodded her head. My wife consoled her and calmed her down, and she was okay very quickly.

Thinking back on it, I realize that it was not a simple single-selection situation. It was an "all of the above" situation. She probably even foresaw that I was going to tell her that I needed to spend time with Ivan, and that she knew that was the right thing to do and she was okay with it, even though it made her sad. She was sobbing but she knew what the right thing was, before I even talked to her. Her brain processed the possible scenarios but she couldn't verbalize her complex feelings and opinions.

Several days later, when I needed to play with Ivan again, I drew a picture, shown below, for Mindy on the magnetic drawing board, asking for her permission. Mindy took the board, wrote down her "OK" response, circled it with a speech bubble, and then read it out loud. That was a most heartwarming moment. (Mindy and Ivan's names have been edited in the image from the original photo.)

Mindy granting permission for me to work with Ivan

Singing

It is safe to say that both Mindy and Ivan learned to sing before they learned to talk. First they sang phonetically, without actual comprehension. Mindy sang in multiple languages: English, Japanese, Thai, Portuguese, Vietnamese, you name it. Back then, she did it based on phonetics, and could memorize some very long songs. When Mindy was a little over three years old, I saw a gradual shift in the way she stored information. She started to show signs of verbal comprehension, and she now stored songs with verbal understanding. That also meant that she was no longer memorizing songs phonetically, so she started to forget her Japanese, Thai, and Portuguese songs.

Anyway, singing is a great bridge to verbalization. It sets up a phonetic foundation. YouTube has an immense collection of good videos of children's songs.

Acting

Another way for children with autism to develop verbal skills is by doing scripted acting. Mindy loved to act like Calvin and Suzie (characters from the *Calvin and Hobbes* series). In one of the strips, Calvin climbed down the bedroom window in the middle of the night, then went to a phone booth and made a call home, "Hello Dad! It is now three in the morning: do you know where I am?" We would take turns playing this scene, climbing down from the edge of the couch. We often also played a scene where Calvin tried to repulse Suzie by telling her that he was having a squid eyeball sandwich for lunch. Mindy sometimes used her toy lamb to emulate Hobbes, but she would replace "tiger" in her script with "sheep," and "Hobbes" with "Lulu." As Mindy's reading skills became more advanced, she could do more complex acting. She loved a video clip about the story of *Hansel and Gretel*, so I wrote the conversation from the video clip as a script, and performed the play with her.

Mindy started to act early. In school, she learned to play doctor. She would play it at home, too, asking us to open our mouths and say "ahhh," and then she would use an invisible stethoscope to check our heartbeats, and at the end would give us an injection. Back then she did not talk much: we mostly played with sound effects, like humming the heartbeat sound. Still, it was fun to play.

Scripted acting (role playing) is a way to encourage your children to engage in more advanced verbal communication situations. While it is scripted, not spontaneous, it still helps your children connect what they already know to new concepts. I find scripted acting helps build a bridge to increased verbalization. It's also a lot of fun for the whole family.

Socialization

Socialization is a touchy point, as it relates to autism. You may have noticed that I have mentioned very little about socialization in this book. This is not a careless omission. My opinion is that the current ABA approach places too much emphasis on socialization. As a person on the spectrum myself, sometimes I feel so frustrated that typical people do not understand us at all.

I still remember my parents' concern. My Mom kept telling me, "How come you don't socialize with people? You need to acquire social skills to be successful in life." I preferred to go hiding whenever there were visitors at home. I was a failure in my parents' eyes. But in school I had many friends. Still, it wasn't until I got into my PhD program, that I realized I was not such a weird kid: there were many more people like me. I do not think I developed into the failed person that my parents have feared. I worked, got married, and am raising a family. And let me not just talk about myself: I have seen many people with far fewer social skills than me who are much more successful in life.

I like to be around people. No one likes to be lonely, not even children with autism. What I really enjoyed the most was being near people, but having my own space to do my thinking. I missed my high school days very much, precisely because it was the ideal environment for me. In my free time, I could sit on the second floor balcony, dangle my legs in the air, and think about life and its meaning. While my friends developed by playing and socializing, I developed by looking inwards on purpose of life and on humans in general. Was I anti-social? Not at all; I always had plenty of friends and participated in all kinds of social activities.

It is hard for me to understand the worries of parents and teachers about children with autism not socializing. I mean, what is the hurry in acquiring social skills? To me, it is better to spend time developing vital intellectual skills for these children, and to let them explore becoming social at their own paces.

I am not against developing socialization skills in children with autism; they do need it. But I am against spending so much time on developing social skills, while neglecting their strengths in visual communication. Without developing their vital intellectual skills, children run the risk of becoming permanently incapacitated. With well-developed vital intellectual skills, these children will shine with their abilities, get good jobs, and contribute to society. Most importantly, they will gain self-confidence and self-esteem. When parents and teachers focus so much on development of these children's social skills, the very skills that would allow these children to be creative and self-confident are often neglected.

I think the root of the issue goes back to the ill-conceived notion that autism is a disease or a disorder. Since many therapists and parents consider autism an illness, they attempt to "cure" it by molding children with autism into the paradigm of typical children. Typical children socialize first, then speak, and then learn to read much later. That's the typical sequence of development. So, many therapists will not attempt to teach children with autism to read before teaching them to verbalize and to socialize. I can understand the concern behind their hesitation: typical children just don't do that!

Typical children: socialization → speech → reading
Children with autism: reading → speech → socialization

Frankly, given the visual way of storing information of children with autism, postponing the development of reading skills adversely impacts the development of their speech and social skills as well. The visual part of the reading process helps build the foundation of memory and brain functions of people with autism. So, by postponing the reading skills, we are effectively postponing all the other skills of these children, including the social part. Worse yet, as a result of the delayed development, these children may suffer self-esteem problems when they start school. There is nothing to gain by intentionally delaying the development of their talents. The only thing we achieve is that by the time these children get into school they compare unfavorably to their typical classmates. There are different ways to succeed in life—not everyone needs to become a professional football player or a movie actress. Not everyone will be

161

the president of a country. Why deny our children leadership roles in the areas where they can be leaders? Why do we turn our children's lives upside-down just to try to meet the standards of typical folks?

We have to keep in mind that children with autism are not typical children, and that they are not sick. They are just different. They belong to a different species and have a different way of learning, a different path of development. We shouldn't force what we consider normal upon these children. We should instead strive to discover their talents and let them develop in the most natural way to them, not the most natural way to us.

My recommendation would be to let socializing skills come naturally. Mindy is now a very social girl with lots of friends, and with excellent leadership skills. She developed her social skills without any intervention on my part. If anything, I contributed to her confidence and assertiveness by helping her develop her reading skills early on, so she could be ahead of her peers in many areas. Her classmates often asked Mindy to read books for them.

Until the day when more therapy techniques address autism, not as a disorder, but as a different path of development, parents are responsible for developing their children's visual-manual skills, including reading, drawing/painting, and building block construction. Parents need to advocate for their children, encouraging therapists and teachers to work together with them for the betterment of their children.

Will My Child Ever Become Normal?

I am keenly aware that the majority of parents, including myself, want their children to develop into balanced and well-rounded people. But we cannot be blind to our children's characteristics and their talents. They belong to a different species: what you think is normal may not be normal to them. We should not impose typical children's standards on children with autism, just as we shouldn't impose a normal animal's behavior on humans. Otherwise, we would all be walking around without clothes on.

My answer to the question, "Will my child ever become normal?" is another question: why would you ever want your child to be normal? Why would you want your child to be the average Joe or the average Jane, when they can be exceptional? Speaking as a person on the spectrum, being autistic is who we are. We are different from typical people, but we are equal-rights human beings. Just because we are different does not mean that we need to turn our lives upside-down trying to meet the same standards as non-autistic people. As more and more people understand autism, the world will become more accommodating. The world will become a better place.

List of Vital Skills

In this last section, I would like to list some skills that I consider vital for children with autism to develop. These are, of course, dependent on the specific circumstances of your child, and their age, and the milestones that they have already reached. I think it will help parents to have a checklist so that when they are thinking about modulating in additional processes, they can get ideas from this list. I recommend that children with autism develop the ability to:

- Pay attention to video clips.
- Handle/withstand light and noise.
- Focus on parents' finger pointing.
- Point to desired objects.
- Focus on simple pictures/drawings.
- Recognize family members in cartoon drawings.
- Imitate animal sounds or equipment sounds (like the vacuum cleaner). Show curiosity about whistling sounds.
- Drink from a cup and use utensils.
- Dance/jump to the rhythm of a song/music.
- Clap hands.
- Hold hands with peers and dance in a circle.
- Correlate songs with body motions, like "The Wheels on the Bus," "Head, Shoulders, Knees, and Toes," "Hokey Pokey," etc.
- Construct objects using building blocks. Pretend play with building blocks.

- Echo words.
- Label objects.
- Say "Mommy" and "Daddy."
- Express needs verbally, as in "I want..."
- Say, "I want water" and "I am hungry." The sign language version counts.
- Play simple two-person games, like running to commands like "go" and "stop," or "fast" and "slow." Also able to go *tap, tap, tap* on a family member and say, "I am a good boy/girl."
- Answer questions, instead of echoing questions.
- Sing songs.
- Count numbers.
- Recognize shapes and colors.
- Read single words.
- Read two-word expressions.
- Do simple phonics exercises and sound out new words.
- Read a sentence.
- Speak with a normal voice, instead of a robotic voice.
- Read a paragraph or a story.
- Parse sentence elements. Also read long sentences without slurring.
- Recognize speech bubbles in cartoon drawings. Know how to speak in turn.
- Protest verbally, as in "I don't like it."
- Have a basic conversation, such as responding to "How are you?" with "I am good." Answer questions like "How old are you?" and "What's your name?"
- Have basic conversations on the telephone, like: "Hello, who is this?" "I am Mindy."
- Read comic books. Imitate a character's emotions and tones.
- Recognize people's emotions from pictures.
- Draw simple shapes.
- Draw simple pictures. Create and tell a brand new story.
- Write letters, and write own name.

- Role-play using imaginary characters or storylines from books or video clips.
- Do simple arithmetic like addition and subtraction. Recognize basic mathematical symbols (+, -, =).
- Defend themselves, as in "Stop it! I am telling the teacher. You need to respect me."
- Use a computer and/or smartphone, including keyboard and mouse skills.
- Ask questions.
- Describe recent events. Story telling.

The list goes on. If your child is receiving services, the ABA case manager or the school district's IEP (Individualized Education Program) may offer additional skill milestones that you may want to consider. Whenever your child is (a) throwing a tantrum, (b) engaging in repetitive behaviors, including stimming, (c) having sensory issues, or (d) acting unengaged/doing nothing, instead of becoming concerned, think positively. Consider which skills your child still needs to learn, and focus your energy on how you can reach your child with your message and help your child to learn. Always think about visual approaches for the delivery of your messages. Your children have a lot of skills to acquire to become successful adults. Your role in their development is too crucial to delegate to nurses, therapists, teachers, or the government. In fact, my wife and I view our home as the foundation for our children's learning. ABA services and schools are there to expand our children's learning, but parent-child interaction is paramount.

I know it takes a lot of effort to draw pictures and make video clips for your children. It also takes to time to search for educational books and video clips, to sit down and read stories with your children, to find out from your children about their daily activities, and about their frustrations. It does take time to communicate with your children and develop their skills. Every day counts. It is a lot of work, but it is totally worth it. I also know it is tempting to sidetrack into fun times or to compensate your children with entertainments. However, the investment of your time and effort in your children's learning will change their future.

In summary, autism is a communication problem. The communication is often broken on our end, not on the children's end. The children are totally capable of learning. We, the adults, are the ones who need to change our behavior.

5

REFLECTIONS ON AUTISM

Different Tunes: on Bugle and Recorder

This section will explore some analogies with autism. I often rely on these types of "models" to help me understand autism and to help find solutions to specific problems when interacting with my children.

Let's face it—the real world is complex. The same thing is true with autism. We have yet to understand its true causes and mechanisms. Scientific inquiries may eventually help us understand this condition better. However, as parents, we want an answer not in five, ten, or twenty years from now—we want the answer yesterday.

This is not to discredit scientific research on autism. Science takes time. Parents simply do not have the luxury of time: each and every day counts. Each day that goes by that the child is not properly developed means a higher risk of the child becoming permanently handicapped.

When we encounter new things or complicated subjects, we invariably try to borrow analogies from things that we already know. That is how human knowledge develops and expands—by building upon what we know. When we use analogies in a consistent and systematic manner, we call it a "model." A model provides us some

167

form of a mental picture to handle the problems that we face on a daily basis. Models are never perfect, but they help us understand the world out there.

The simplest "model" of autism that I have been able to find is inspired from my exposure to musical instruments.

When I was a little boy, my sister started to take piano lessons. We, the two younger brothers, excitedly told our parents that we also wanted to learn to play piano. We did not know that learning to play the piano required patience. To make a long story short, my brother lasted three weeks, and I lasted six weeks, before we both gave up piano lessons.

That was my entire formal training on musical instruments. Later, I had opportunities to play around with wind instruments, too. I cannot remember where I found it or got it, but I played with a small bugle. I later also learned to play the recorder, or "flauta dulce" as it is known in Spanish.

The interesting thing about the bugle is that it is very simple yet it can make multiple sounds. A bugle does not have any keys or control valves. You just blow into it for the note you want to make, and your note will be amplified through the horn.

(I know at this point the real experts on wind instruments would jump in and correct me with words like "harmonic series" and things like that. But this is a book about autism, not about musical instruments. Also, we are talking about models here.)

Another simple instrument, at least in terms of design, is the recorder, which is basically a pipe with multiple holes drilled on it. Let's assume for now that all the holes are blocked with your fingers. No matter what note you try to blow into the recorder, the note that comes out is always the same. It does not work like a bugle. You cannot control a recorder by telling it what note to play with your mouth/lip. The recorder does not obey the command of your mouth/lip. You can only make the notes change by opening or blocking the holes.

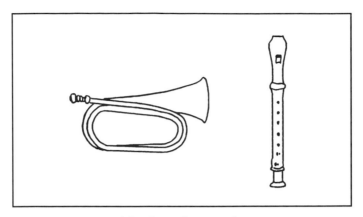

A bugle and a recorder

Where am I going with all this?

- Typical children are like bugles: they resonate with your verbal commands and understand you easily.
- Children with autism are like recorders: they have their own minds. They are stuck on a single note (stimming). They do not understand your verbal commands.

If you keep trying to play a recorder the way you play a bugle, you will get frustrated. You will get a single note, and you will get annoyed to no end. However, does this mean that a recorder is a failure as a musical instrument? Not at all. It just requires a different playing approach. When we learn to "modulate" the recorder by opening and blocking its outlet holes properly, it can play very nice music. The key is to learn its modulation techniques.

Children with autism are no different. Some important messages I would like you to draw from the recorder analogy are:

- Do not get stuck on your children's stimming behavior. Their repetitive behavior is a fundamental building block of their thought process. Do not censor their fundamental expression. Let them express themselves.
- The only message your children want you to understand with their repetitive behavior is, "This is the door to my

169

world, please come on in." Do not waste time analyzing their behavior or trying to find an explanation, just as you shouldn't waste time in wondering why a recorder doesn't play like a bugle.

- Your children are perfectly capable of learning. You just need to modulate your message around their main note. Once you master the modulation technique, you will soon hear music from them!

Radio Circuits

My next model for autism is inspired from my childhood hobby of assembling radio circuits.

I started playing with electronic circuits when I was nine years old. By today's standard, that is considered late.

Not too long ago, I ordered a crystal radio kit by mail for my nephew Tin. I had to laugh when I opened the package. The instructions stated: "Not suitable for children under three." So there you go. Welcome to the new world.

I have to give my parents credit for their tolerance for my hobby. I had a classmate and also an uncle who introduced me to the world of electronic circuits. After assembling my first crystal radio, I learned to solder electronic components. To scavenge for electronic components, I disassembled my parent's wedding gift: a vintage AM radio with a record player. It surely caused quite a bit of commotion when my parents saw their memorabilia torn to pieces. I am glad that they were magnanimous and did not punish me. I assembled various radio circuits: first with vacuum tubes and then with transistors. I also followed some circuit manual and built a radio transmitter. Then I started to broadcast my own radio program to my neighborhood, music included. Back then, Taiwan was under martial law. My radio transmissions got my father into big trouble. They thought the transmitter belonged to my father and that my father was into some secret revolutionary organization...Luckily around that time we moved to South America, before I caused further trouble for my parents. One thing I did appreciate about Taiwan was that it was the kingdom of electronic components. There were a few electronic component stores within walking distance of my home.

I have fond memories from my circuit-boy days. Even today, every time I see a vacuum tube, I still feel so much nostalgia…It is like seeing a long lost friend again.

One of the circuits I assembled in the early days was a "regenerative radio." Wikipedia has a nice diagram for the regenerative receiver circuit, which I reproduced below under its public domain permission.

I know some of you readers may be aghast at my including a radio circuit diagram in a book on autism. But please remember that I am autistic, so please bear with me and forgive my unusual approach…The circuit analogy has been my primary source of ideas for approaching autism.

The regenerative receiver circuit gave me insight into the autistic mind. I explain in simple terms its more relevant features. Once the radio signal is captured by the antenna (on the top-left corner of the diagram), the signal is processed by the vacuum tube (the big circle at the middle of the diagram). One very cool feature about the regenerative circuits is that the output of the vacuum tube goes into a "tickler" coil, which completes a positive, reinforced feedback loop to the incoming radio signal. What does this mean? The signal of radio waves is very faint. We are bathed in radio waves on a permanent basis. These radio signals do not cause any harm to us precisely because they are so weak. That being said, for a radio receiver to work properly and convert these faint signals into something that people can actually hear, the signals must be amplified. The regenerative circuit is clever in that it uses one single vacuum tube to amplify the signal multiple times. This feature is what gives us its namesake: regenerative. So, the amplified output of the vacuum tube is actually fed back to its input, achieving a compounded effect on signal amplification.

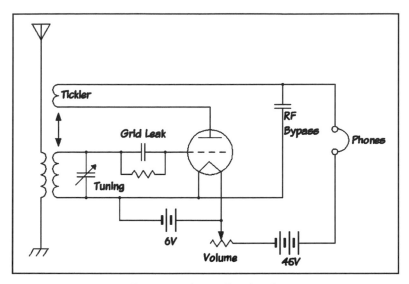

Regenerative radio circuit

One nuisance of a regenerative radio is that, when it is not properly tuned to the frequency of a radio station, it will enter into an overdriven feedback loop. The same principle is used in something called the Armstrong Oscillator circuit. See the next figure, again taken from Wikipedia under its public domain permission. In fact, one of the dangers of a regenerative radio is that the feedback loop is so strong that it can effectively become a transmitter and affect other electronic equipment nearby.

What does the regenerative radio circuit analogy tell us about autism?

(a)　Autism is most likely not due to poor connections inside the brain. On the contrary, children with autism seem to have "overdriven" connections inside their brains. It is not the lack of connections that drive these children into resonance oscillation (stimming), but rather, it is the presence of powerful feedback-loop connections that drive these children into their autistic behavior.

(b)　When the input signal is properly modulated as it is in the case of the radio station signal, the regenerative circuit is able to properly respond. Not only that, due to the powerful

172

feedback loop, the circuit is actually able to detect very minuscule details. The same thing is true with children with autism. When our communication to them is properly "modulated," not only can these children respond properly, but often they will surprise us with their powerful brains.

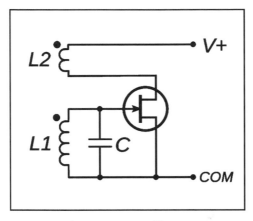

Armstrong oscillator

In all likelihood, the autistic brain is a powerful brain. The keywords nowadays seem to be "hyper-connectivity," "brain overgrowth," and "excess synapses," and many research papers have been published along these lines.

Now that we know a bit more about autism, I cannot but feel sorry about how mistreated these children have been in the past. We have essentially trashed so many bright minds due to our lack of understanding. Take the case of Victor of Aveyron for instance, a presumed "feral child" found in France at the turn of the nineteenth century. Victor, according to modern-day French surgeon Serge Aroles, was an example of a child with autism who was abused and then abandoned to the wilderness. Likewise, until recently, it was common practice to institutionalize children with more severe forms of autism. Although these dreadful stories are now behind us, vestiges of the stigma still remain. From time to time I still see in the news mistreatment of children with autism. I sincerely hope that our society can start to view our children with autism as great assets, develop them in a way that is natural to them, and provide them with an environment where they can contribute with their talents. I am glad that some large companies such as SAP and Freddie Mac have started to consider autistic traits positively in their hiring of certain positions. So I am optimistic about the future.

I can get carried away with drawing ideas from various circuit analogies. For example, I could go on and talk about "super-heterodyne" radio and how it led me to think about the role of meditation, chanting, or background music in helping adults with autism. I could go on with another interesting circuit known as the "reflex radio," which provided me with insight into a strange phenomenon known as "synesthesia" observed in some people with autism. I could go on and talk about non-linear effects analogous to singing with an overtone dual voice. I could talk about schizophrenia, which some researchers now consider as an extension of autism. But I think I will keep it simple and stop here.

What is Autism, Then?

While I was writing this book, I acquired a more consistent picture about autism. I came to realize that autistic characteristics like apathy, stimming, sensory problems, and even "savant" abilities, all had a common root.

I believe that autism arises due to (a) over-connectivity of brain cells, and (b) a strong feedback loop in brain activities due to the increased connectivity. So to put it into an equation:

Autism = Unmitigated auto-feedback due to an overly-connected brain.

In a sense, autism arises because the brains of these children are just *too* powerful. Unmitigated, these children will be left resonating in their inner world and may even become permanently disabled. With proper modulation and communication, these children can thrive in their development and will do wonders.

In my opinion, autism does not mean a lack of connections inside the brain. Children with autism have all the wiring in place for verbal skills and for socializing skills. Their brains are not damaged.

174

However, due to the powerful auto-feedback loops they are on, they focus on the visual-manual channels. The right way to develop these children is not by forcing them to use their weak channels of verbal and socialization skills. Doing so only causes more harm than good. Let these children develop through their natural channels first, and they will surprise you by building up their verbal and social skills much faster. Please do not turn the lives of these children upside down. They have a different path of growth.

Let me give a personal example. In Minnan Chinese, my native dialect, there is a hard *g* sound that I found impossible to make. I never learned to pronounce it, even when I was twelve years old. That year, we moved to South America and I learned to speak Spanish. Spanish has the same hard *g* sound, and I picked it up with no trouble whatsoever. So I could finally speak my own dialect correctly, too. What my parents had failed to teach me for about ten years, I mastered within one day. What made the difference? I learned Spanish visually (meaning learning its alphabet first), instead of aurally. The visual channel made the difference. (As with most Chinese dialects, my dialect is almost never written: not even in phonetic form.) What is the moral of my story? The quickest path may not always be the typical path. The difference, in this case, was the difference between ten years and one day. If you can understand this example, you can understand how to communicate with the autistic species. Let go of what you've learned is the "normal path," and start to think like a person with autism. In my particular case, was I unable to learn? Did I have neurological problems? Or was the problem that the type of communication used to teach me to learn was not the right one, until I was twelve years old? Ten years or one day: I think the answer is clear.

Traditional Approach vs. Eikona Bridge

The following table provides a summary of the main differences between Eikona Bridge and the traditional approach toward interacting with children with autism.

Topic	Traditional Approach	Eikona Bridge
Autism is…	a behavioral problem.	a communication problem.
Tantrums happen because of…	a behavioral problem.	a communication problem. You solve the communication problem, and everything else will fall in place.
Stimming and repetitive behaviors…	must be "corrected" or suppressed.	are the children's way of telling you "This is the door to my world, please come on in!" Use stimming and repetitive behaviors as Archimedes' lever to teach children new vital skills. Repetitive behaviors will either subside, or allow you to teach your children further skills.
Communicate…	through their ears.	through their eyes.
Social interaction is…	the top priority. Typical children learn everything from social interaction.	not a priority. Intellectual development is the top priority. Offer opportunities for social interaction, but let it develop naturally.

Normalcy	Children with autism are sick; they must be treated to become normal.	Children with autism are special gifts to the world; they should never be forced to become normal.
Attention deficit disorder	Children with autism suffer from attention deficit disorder.	Children with autism do not suffer from attention deficit disorder. They can focus very well on personalized cartoon pictures and/or video clips.
Hyperactivity	Hyperactive children can't learn. Prescription drugs are often indicated.	Children with high energy levels do not need medication, but rather a mix of work with play, and communication through their visual language.
Speech	Children with autism must learn to speak, because verbal communication is the typical way to learn other skills.	Children with autism should learn to read first. Talking will come naturally. Build their self-confidence by leveraging their exceptional visual-manual skills.

Academics (school curricula such as reading, math, science, etc.)	Academics are excluded from treatment, which focuses on behavioral improvement. Academics are considered the responsibility of schools. However, schools scale teaching of academic skills to the levels of typical classmates, which means that children with autism are often delayed in development of skills like reading and writing, skills which significantly improve their communication ability.	Academics are integral to the Eikona Bridge philosophy. There is no reason to delay teaching advanced academic skills to children with autism because these skills open additional channels of communication. There is no reason to delay finding out that a non-verbal child can communicate through typing.
IEP (Individualized Education Plan)	Children with autism use a structured education plan tailored to each individual student by schools, but the plans focus on typical skill sets taught in a typical order, which means that the skills they need most, like reading and writing, are taught to them too late.	Children with autism should be required through IEPs to learn visual communication skills earlier than typical classmates, particularly in reading, drawing, and computer skills (such as typing, image editing, and computer programming).

Sensory problems...	are best handled by avoiding stimuli, wearing protective gear, and/or medicating.	are best handled by modulating additional activities to broaden these sensitive "Dirac deltas." Connecting old processes to new ones will improve children's understanding of their environment and tolerance of problematic stimuli. The sensory problems will go away by themselves.
Empathy	Children with autism are not capable of caring about other people. Empathy must be developed.	Children with autism view everyone as an equal, so they care about everyone when they grow up. They are superb team players. Empathy, like social interaction, does not need to be emphasized as an immediate developmental priority.
Self-esteem...	is achieved by making these children "normal" as soon as possible, so that they acclimate to societal norms and standards for their age groups.	Is achieved by developing the special talents of these children, and letting them realize their own strengths, so they won't need to rely on their peers' opinions.

Who is sick?	Children with autism	Shifts away from viewing autism as a disorder, and raises awareness in parents, teachers, and adults in general on how to interact with children from this "new species."
Who needs behavioral correction?	Children with autism	Shifts away from viewing autism as a behavioral issue, and emphasizes on developing communication skills for all children, parents, teachers and adults in general.
Domain of autism assistance	Healthcare	Special education

Can Typical Children Benefit from Eikona Bridge?

I'll be frank: I don't know.

I just don't know whether the way people with autism think and learn can be applied to typical children at an early age. I am pretty certain that at a later age, meaning middle school and above, both camps (typical and autistic) have developed enough intellectual skills that they can learn from the same sources. But at an earlier age, I am not sure whether the autistic approach can resonate with typical children.

Let me clarify. I have shown some of my video clips for Ivan to my adult friends. Most of them cannot stand watching them beyond one or two minutes. They are totally unable to relate to the messages in the clips. In other words, my video clips do not resonate at all with non-autistic adults. Whether the same is true for non-autistic young children, I just don't know. My suspicion is that the same holds true.

Instead of using the learning techniques meant for children with autism to educate typical children, I have a better suggestion. The Montessori education program uses an approach that works well for both autistic and typical children, because it emphasizes visual and sensory development, and respects the individuality of each child. I would recommend the Montessori route for typical children if parents have the desire to develop their children from a visual-sensory-individualistic standpoint.

Low-Functioning vs. High-Functioning

One aspect that I have not touched so far is the distinction between low- and high-functioning forms of autism. This is not a careless omission. I know some readers may get the wrong impression that this is book is only about high-functioning children with autism, since I keep talking about developing their talents. But that is not the case, and let me elaborate.

The truth is, I have met with what people might call low-functioning children. I have looked into their eyes, and I simply cannot call them "low-functioning." I can see the sparkle in their eyes. I cannot forget one particular instance. As I started to draw some pictures for a low-functioning teenage boy with autism, his eyes just glued to what I was drawing. He did not blink. I felt as if there was a laser beam coming out of his eyes, such was the intensity of his focus.

I have never seen a single child on the spectrum that I would describe as having "low-functioning autism." I am not in denial: I have met "low-functioning" people with autism with a wide range of ages. I simply do not believe in the existence of a distinction between low-functioning autism and high-functioning autism. As an outcome of development, yes, I do accept that some children grow up to be high-functioning persons and some others may turn into low-functioning persons. But as for the inherent nature of autism, I do not see a low-high distinction. I see all children with autism as capable of thriving in their development and becoming successful adults, if only we communicate with them properly in their language.

What I do see is a distinction between pro-video and pro-picture children. Some readers may be tempted to identify pro-video children as more low-functioning, but this is simply not the case. If you ask me, I personally admire more the brains of pro-video children: they can see things that I can't see, and they can do things that I can't do. Some pro-video adults are much more successful in life than their typical peers.

As I view autism as a communication problem, instead of saying this child is low-functioning and that child is high-functioning, I would rather describe them as "less well understood" and "better understood." The children are fine the way they are. The responsibility for understanding and communicating resides with us, the adults.

Why Such an Unusual Perspective?

My perspective on autism is probably unusual to many readers. Since I am autistic, it's a given that I am not typical, and neither are my ideas. I also understand this book can be perceived as unconventional: in what other books on autism will you find radio circuits, Fourier transforms, Dirac deltas, and convolution/modulation? Also, I have not seen books on autism so sprinkled with cartoon drawings. I have always found that strange—so many books talk about the visual nature of children with autism, but so few books actually include visual representations of autistic understandings. But, just as with most autistic persons, there is a rationale behind their quirkiness. And let me try to explain where I come from.

A buzzword often used in autism research is the "evidence-based" approach. I am a theoretical particle physicist by training. The evidence-based approach may sound very authoritative to people not trained in science, but to a theoretical particle physicist like me it sounds like the nineteenth century way of doing science. It's not a wrong way of approaching science. For things like pharmaceutical drug research, it is still the tried-and-true approach. And in physics we also say no theory should be trusted until verified by an experiment. That is all fair.

That being said, there was a big breakthrough in theoretical physics around 1920 or so. With the advent of Relativity Theory and Quantum Mechanics, particularly after the establishment of Quantum Field Theory, theoretical physicists started to develop science in a different fashion. Gradually, they realized that our world is dictated by very elegant mathematical constructions, known as Lagrangians. I would say before the reign of the Lagrangian field-theoretical approach, physicists were doing things pretty much like everyone else: with an evidence-based, bottom-up approach. That was precisely why Relativity and Quantum Mechanics were not very well-received during their initial era: all too many people were clung to the old bottom-up, evidence-based paradigm. After the Lagrangian field theoretical approach became well-known, physicists opened the floodgates and started to develop theories in a very different way. Instead of spending time going first through the details of a multitude of experiments out there, they now focused first on what other advanced mathematical constructions are possible. Now it was a top-down approach. Yes, physicists still tried to gather clues from symmetries in experimental observations, but those symmetries would now merely provide the necessary inspiration. They then constructed their theories from the top down, made predictions, and then verified them with experiments.

What I find messy in the current autism literature is that everything is so fragmented. That is a typical problem of the evidence-based, bottom-up approach. One misses the forest because of staring too much at the trees: it is very hard to see the big picture. Socially, the bottom-up approach lends itself to non-stop nitpicking, treating science like courtroom drama until everyone loses the big picture.

I chose the top-down approach, instead. I preferred to start with a mental picture of the autistic brain and from there developed all the implications and solutions. The top-down approach is the reason I view stimming and sensory problems as a single unified phenomenon. That is how I identified the concepts of Dirac delta and white noise in children with autism. That is how I arrived at the conclusion that modulation is the key to teaching children with autism. That is why I stress the need for them to learn to read before talking. And that is why I suggest a prioritization of intellectual development over the development of social skills.

So, in my train of thought, there is the Lagrangian field theoretical mind-set working behind the scenes. You may find my approach to autism unconventional. Most people would even call it controversial, especially with regard to my (a) view that autism is a communication problem instead of a behavioral problem, (b) view that children with autism are problem-free and parents and teachers are the ones who need behavioral correction, (c) insistence that reading goes before talking, and (d) placement of priority on the development of intellectual skills before social skills. Whenever I confront the many issues related to children with autism, inside my mind I always keep the picture of Brain City's traffic grid. I think about how to best direct the energy flow in our brain's wiring, and make connection after connection.

Unfortunately, there are not many other good, relatable examples of doing science using a top-down approach except from modern theoretical physics. The method is pretty unique to this realm of science. It is probably the only area where people can get away with developing something like string theory without being called insane. When it comes to my perspective about autism, I agree with all those qualifiers such as "unusual," "unconventional," and "controversial." Trust me, as a physicist, you get used to hearing those terms. You learn to become numb to those comments and just keep plowing ahead. When strangers come and tell me "Your children are always happy!" that is my reward.

So, yes, there is more behind my approach to autism. And I am grateful to my teachers, professors, colleagues and friends—I learned so much from them. They have made my understanding of autism possible. In a sense, they helped my children, too, even though they were not aware of it. There is a quote from the ancient Chinese "Book of Odes" that says **"Stones from other hills may serve to polish the jade of this one."** And I truly believe that there is further room for an exchange of ideas between exact sciences and social sciences.

"Stones from other hills may serve to polish the jade of this one."
An ancient quote that captures the essence of "modulation."
We can bring out the best in us, when we leverage on others,
From *Shijing*, the Chinese *Book of Odes*, circa 800 CE

Coming Age of the Autistic Species

I think of the presence of the autistic species as being here on Earth on some special mission. What that mission is, exactly, I don't know, but I can offer a line of thought.

Humanity faces a large number of challenges in the near future, things like a lack of viable alternative sources of energy, overpopulation and overexploitation, climate changes, potential asteroid collision with the earth, and the list goes on. These challenges pose serious threats to humanity. In addition, humans seem to be more and more self-serving, despite the increasing need to consider the future of humanity as a whole. The Great Recession of 2009 brought to light our selfishness. More and more people are into "making money fast" games. Income inequality is worsening. The aging of our population is also like a time bomb waiting to explode. Social conflicts seem unavoidable in the future.

The things is, society advances only when people are willing to make sacrifices, work hard, and care about other people. If too many people are into taking shortcuts, into zero-sum games, into "make money fast" schemes, into "you do the work, I get the free ride," what happens next is innovation stalls, the economy collapses, and everyone suffers. There is no mystery in recession. Recession happens when society as a whole has wasted time in non-productive activities. When many selfish people are unwilling to put in honest work, society suffers.

I think that is where the autistic species is like a breath of fresh air. Unlike their typical peers, the autistic species stands out through selflessness: (a) they are driven by their desire to improve the good of the entire community with their actions, not just with their words, and (b) they care about other people, not just their own autistic species, but all of humanity. They can better focus on the big picture.

I also believe that we are experiencing the coming age of the autistic species because of the arrival of robotic technology. After the Internet and smartphones, I believe that robots will contribute to the next phase of the economic revolution. I am not talking about industrial robots. I am talking about household robots and workplace robots. When robots can perform the many mundane tasks that are performed by humans today, we will be left to wonder what value humans still have. I have discussed this issue with my scientist friends. From my vantage point, humans remain valuable because we can do (a) non-stop learning and on-the-spot learning, and (b) non-stop creativity: pulling rabbits out of a hat. These are skills that our future economy will depend on. And I believe these are the areas where the autistic species can excel. Our society needs to evolve. I believe the autistic species can show us the way forward.

EPILOGUE

So this book is written. And I am feeling many complex emotions.

First of all, I feel like this book has two volumes: one visible, and one invisible. It took two people to raise our children. What you have read is the visible volume, written by me. What you have not read is the invisible volume, written by my wife with her love for our children and for our entire family. I apologize for not getting more into my wife's part. We both work hard side-by-side to raise our children, and she is the unsung hero. Just remember that without her persistent push, this book would not have seen daylight. She has made tremendous sacrifices to help our children and family, for which I am deeply grateful.

Second, I know very well that this book has been harsh on parents. But please remember I am a parent, too. I can beat myself up all I want for understanding my boy late in the game. None of the concepts that inspired me to develop the Eikona Bridge approach are new. I learned about Fourier transforms some thirty years ago. I did multimedia software development fifteen years ago. I understood aspect-oriented programming ten years ago. Yet for two and a half years I failed to help my own boy. So please excuse my harshness, as it comes from a sense of regret and guilt I carry. And the only thing I can tell myself is better late than never. To the parents of children with autism, no matter how old your children are, look ahead and make up for lost time. This is not a book about tears. This is a book about joy and laughter. My children have taught me to laugh. Their laughter has made all the hard work worth it.

Summary

To recap this book: the underlying messages of Eikona Bridge are not complicated.

1) My first message is: do not worry needlessly. That does not mean you shouldn't do something for your children. Children with autism require more work from their parents. However, most of worries from parents are misplaced. Since I am myself autistic, I do get access to "insider information," and I often get frustrated to see parents and therapists worrying about things that are not important to the development these children. Children with autism belong to a different species, and they have their own developmental path. Mindy and Ivan constantly receive praise from teachers and other parents as being "happy kids," something that is often hard to believe since both of them are clinically diagnosed with autism. I do not claim to hold the "secret sauce" to solve all the issues of autism, but one thing that has helped in the development of Mindy and Ivan is that I did not needlessly worry about their condition. My advice to parents is: do not view autism as a disease or a defect. These children are special in their own way. When you worry that your children are not behaving like typical children, you drain your energy in helpless tactics, which often end up causing harm in your relationship with your children. Worry-free parents mean happy kids.

2) Identify your children's type of autism. Decide whether your children are pro-picture (picture-memory based) or pro-video (video-memory based). The key differentiation is whether they can focus on static pictures. Draw some pictures in front of their eyes. If they can focus on your drawing and react to it, then they are pro-picture. Otherwise, they are likely to be pro-video.

188

3) Communicate with your children visually. You need to communicate through their eyes, not through their ears. Visual communication brings you much closer to your children's inner world. They will appreciate it.

4) For pro-video children, you need to identify your children's interests and produce some video clips accordingly. Then modulate those video clips with short bursts of "commercials" containing your main messages. As for pro-picture children, you can go straight to the magnetic drawing board. Prepare their picture-based daily diaries. At nighttime, before going to bed, spend time with your children in picture-aided talking. Review what they have done today, and prepare them for what's coming tomorrow. Identify the causes of their frustration. Use speech bubbles to introduce your children to verbal communication.

5) Although it may seem counter-intuitive, my experience tells me that for children with autism, reading must come before talking. This is especially important for pro-video children: only a solid foundation in reading will help them avoid slurring later in life. If your children are not talking, please remember to follow "Read first. Talking can wait." Your children are visual: reading will actually help them talk sooner.

6) Similarly, provide your children with building block toys, and develop their drawing skills as soon as it becomes practical. Once your children can produce manual-visual outputs, they will be able to complete their own outer feedback loop, and start developing deep thinking skills.

7) Always treat your children as equal-rights human beings. Forgo all attempts at manipulation and/or using sugar-coated lies.

8) For repetitive behaviors, participate with your children, but try to "modulate in" additional activities, so they can learn

new skills. Do not suppress repetitive behaviors. Use the 4x6 card albums to show your children the sequence of activities and set expectations. Once they learn other skills from the additional activities, the repetitive behaviors will go away by themselves. Remember Archimedes' lever: your children have provided you with a place to stand; now it's up to you to move the earth.

9) For pro-video children, do not attempt to modify their established processes, even if you think there are mistakes. Instead, start brand new processes to teach them additional skills or to correct their mistakes. This is also true for their speech problems. There is no need to correct isolated mistakes. Instead, introduce them to new sentences. Make it fun; make it into a new game.

10) Remember that autism is a communication problem, not a behavioral problem. Behavioral problems are symptoms of communication problems. You need to track down the root of communication problems. Once you address the communication problems, the behavioral problems will go away by themselves. Children are not born to throw tantrums or be violent. Use pictures and video clips and talk to your children in their native language. Sit down with your children and cross out those negative marks in the double-entry ledger inside their brains. Do not postpone communicating with your children. Seize the moment, and don't let those negative marks become permanent. Help your children to keep faith in humanity.

11) Finally, remember the **LIVE** acronym. This book is entirely about *LIVE* communication with your children: you communicate with your children through Letters, Images, Voice, and Experience. If you keep this acronym in your heart, you will have already come a long way. The *LIVE* communication technique is your Archimedes' lever: that is how you get into your children's inner world.

Support for Children with Autism

Let me outline also my thoughts about autism support today and be clear about a few things. There is no question that children with autism need services: the earlier the intervention, the better. There is also no question that only a clinical psychologist is qualified to determine whether a child has autism. There are just too many varieties of developmental disorders, so a medical professional is needed to make the right evaluation. There is also no question that severe cases of autism may require additional medical help. In short, autism cannot be separated from medical science.

That being said, there is room for debate on our current approach towards autism. Frankly, for the majority of autism cases, I think they fall more under the umbrella of special education. For these cases, autism is more about learning and about communication, than about a medical condition. It is not just me, but as with most adults with autistic traits, we do not want to be "cured" from autism. Being autistic is who we are. We are fully functioning members of society, and we are not "disabled" to any reasonable measure. Most of us work, make a living, and many of us have raised families. Some have even contributed greatly to the progress of humankind. Autism falls into the grey area between healthcare and special education, and it is debatable whether the resources should come from the right hand or from the left hand.

As I have repeatedly pointed out in this book, one quality of people with autism is that they care about humankind as a whole. We care about other people, whether they are autistic or not. We do not spin issues around for personal benefit or for the sole benefit of the autistic community. So let's be objective and try to figure out the best way to go forward, for society as a whole. There is much work to be done.

As I said, I have never shed a single tear over my children's conditions. I have had fun, I have laughed. I feel terribly sorry for involving my children in this book, though. Blame it on my wife, because she was the one who insisted that I write this book. That being said, my wife believes that my message will help many families out there, and I sincerely hope so, too. So my apologies to Mindy and Ivan, but I hope you children take pride in helping other people through your own stories.

And I thank you, the reader, for taking the time to read this book. I hope that you have learned more about how to communicate with the members of the autistic species. Together, we can make this a better world.

Jason H.J. Lu
August, 2014

Singing a lullaby to Mindy

Lullaby from an Old, Old Man

Lullaby from an Old, Old Man
(Arrullo de un Viejo Viejito)

Érase un viejo viejito, de lejos él vino.
"Palabras tengo", él dijo, "me quedo contigo".
Amaneció, atardeció, misma canción cantó.
Amaneció, atardeció, mismo cuento siguió.

There once was a really old, old man, he came from far away.
He said he had some words to share, and he would like to stay.
From the dawn, through the night, his song went on the same.
From the dawn, through the night, his words came back again.

- - - - -

"Hey, who is the old man?"
"That's you, Daddy. You are old, and I am young!"
"Where does the old man come from?"
"Chile, that's your country. My country is U.S.A."
"And what does the old man want to do?"
"He wants to stay in my house!"
"All right. He just wants to stay in your heart, OK?"
"OK."
"Nite nite, sleep tight."
"Nite nite."

…Mindy, Ivan, and Tisa: I love you all.

GLOSSARY

ABA: Applied Behavioral Analysis, a well-known treatment approach for children with autism.

Academics: refers to school curricula, such as reading, math, science, etc. This term is often used as counterpart to "behavioral treatment." Typically, school districts hold exclusivity on teaching academics, meaning that behavioral therapists are not allowed to participate in this area of responsibility.

Coordinate Space/Momentum Space: the two information spaces associated to Fourier Transforms. When presented in a two-dimensional x-y plot, the horizontal x dimension is the coordinate space, and the vertical y dimension is the momentum space.

CPU: Central Processing Unit, a microprocessor in a computer that executes program instructions. CPUs are often used as analogy to human brains.

Double-Entry Ledger: a bookkeeping journal used by accountants. It symbolizes the way children with autism track positive and negative experiences inside their brains. When parents accumulate a negative point in their children's double-entry ledger, the way to cancel it out is by doing picture talking with these children.

Dirac Delta: a mathematical concept, representing a pointlike concentration of information.

Fourier Transform: a reversible mathematical transformation between two worlds, akin to attempting to describe nouns with adjectives, or vice-versa. For instance, a noun such as "tiger" could be described as "feline", "scary", "striped", "carnivorous", etc. Partial correlations are possible, for instance, for "tiger", the descriptors "yellow" and "black" are split 50-50.

Modulation: a technique used in electronic signal processing, to transmit an information signal by porting it through a carrier signal. In this book, modulation has been applied to teaching vital skills to children with autism, by leveraging their favorite repetitive behaviors or video clips. Modulation can also be applied to eliminating sensory problems.

P & P: Planned and purposeful. Refers to intentional repetitions with the purpose of achieving perfection, as opposed to stimming-style repetitions that don't have a clear purpose.

Shadow: an adult aide that accompanies a child with autism in school. The role of a shadow is to facilitate the child's learning experience and to alleviate the burden of teachers.

Stim/Stimming: stands for "self-stimulation," with "to stim" as its verbal form. This term refers to the repetitive behaviors observed in people with autism.

Typical/Neurotypical: stands for non-autistic children.

Outer Feedback Loop: refers to the mechanism by which humans generate extracorporeal signals that are then reabsorbed. For neurotypical children, they can hear their own speech. For pro-picture children, they can draw pictures to close this loop. For pro-video children, they can play with building blocks to accomplish feedback. Only after children close their outer feedback loops, can they start to acquire deep-reasoning skills.

White Noise: a broad-spectrum distribution of information; the opposite of Dirac delta. White noise represents something that is incomprehensible. The word "white" here does not refer to the color, but simply to a mixture of frequencies. Strictly speaking, white noise is a random signal, and not a true opposite partner of Dirac delta. So there is some abuse of mathematical language in this book.

ABOUT THE AUTHOR

Jason H.J. Lu was trained as a theoretical physicist. He received his PhD in 1992 from Stanford University. Jason currently works as a data scientist. Jason enjoys interacting with people from all cultural backgrounds.

Made in the USA
San Bernardino, CA
10 October 2014